Stev

MW01285617

Under a Poacher's Moon 2

Steven Dewald

Steven Dewald

ISBN -10:1484010493

ISBN-13:978-1484010495

Steven Dewald

Steven Dewald

Table of Contents

Steven Dewald

1 Decision at a Fork in the Road

In the summer of 1980, I was a recent graduate of UW-River Falls with a land management degree. Although I had applied for at least 25 full-time jobs, no job offers had been received. It was a difficult economic time in our country as extremely high interest rates slowed business activity and tax revenues. Home loans at the time were available at 18 ½ percent annual rates of interest. The entire country was slipping into recession.

I was fortunate to at least have a summer job. It was my fourth summer working at Kohler Andrae State Park just south of Sheboygan. The park had an exceptional beach with more than a mile of sand shoreline along Lake Michigan. It also had a campground with 105 sites.

Because of the camping, the park had an overnight population similar to many small towns. With that population came along the normal law enforcement challenges any small town police force has to deal with including drunk driving, domestic disputes, traffic violations, and noise complaints. However in contrast to small police departments, the park relied on college students with law enforcement credentials to enforce the law. Due to the significant acreage of the property which included large expanses of sand dunes and forest, it also tended to attract groups of teenagers for underage drinking parties.

My first summer working in the park was in 1977. I was hired to do basic park maintenance that included cleaning buildings, mowing lawns, picking up garbage, and registering campers. During the second summer in 1978, the park manager asked me if I wanted to do law enforcement in the park at night. "Law enforcement," I asked? "You mean arrest people?" I wasn't too sure that was something I was interested in since I was a quiet young man at the time. However the park manager encouraged me to try it.

He advised me that the Department would send me to one week of law enforcement training at Fox Valley Technical School in Appleton to learn about the constitution, search and seizure and the basic legal responsibilities of a law enforcement officer. He described this as "phase training" where park enforcement officers would receive one week of police school each summer they worked at the park, until they had the 6 weeks of training needed to be a certified full-time officer. At that point, the Wisconsin Training and Standards Board would allow the individual to carry a firearm and to be a certified officer at any law enforcement agency in the state. With only one week of training, however, the officer would receive law enforcement credentials with arrest power only on state land. No firearms could be carried.

As I pondered my options I thought law enforcement might be more interesting than cleaning bathrooms or driving the garbage truck so I agreed to take the law enforcement training. After a week in Appleton, I went back to work at the park. One of the full-time rangers took me out on patrol with him for one night. The next night they turned me loose on the park alone since I was considered adequately trained at that point. The entire list of law enforcement equipment issued to me included a flashlight, a set of handcuffs, and a portable radio that sent out a weak signal that the Sheriff's Department dispatcher in Sheboygan could hear about half the time.

Armed only with those three items, I began my law enforcement career working the night shift alone most nights. I would usually be assigned a 6pm to 2am shift or a weekend shift of 8pm to 4am. The most common violation in the park consisted of park curfew violations in which people who were not registered campers would stay in the park after the 11pm curfew. These people were subject to a citation for the offense. The curfew rule was needed to get the partiers out of the park at a reasonable hour so registered campers could get some sleep.

The first citation I issued was to a man for the park curfew violation. As I wrote down his information in my pocket notebook, he informed me he was going to come back in the park later that night with a couple of his friends to beat the crap out of me. My knees were literally bouncing off each other as I wrote down the information. I was not sure at that point if this law enforcement business was such a great idea.

And yet, over the next months and the next two summers at the park, my confidence in my law enforcement abilities grew. Various new experiences gave me a broader understanding of law enforcement. I soon realized that officers could not predict what situations they would encounter during their assigned shift. One day during my first summer of law enforcement, I received a radio call from the park office to check on a possible dead woman on the north beach area. A person walking on the beach had observed a woman face down on the sand who was motionless. I went to the scene with some trepidation. I had never encountered a dead person before.

I easily found the woman. Like the caller had suggested, she was face down in the sand and was not moving. Nor did I see any movement from normal breathing. At that time I had not received any kind of first responder training, so I simply gave the woman a light kick in her thigh to see if there was a response. There was none. I thought to myself, well maybe she is dead. I decided I better make sure so this time I bent down and shook the woman and surprisingly she moaned. I rolled her on to her back. Sand was encrusted in her mouth and nostrils. I was finally able to get her to respond. It became obvious she was very intoxicated. She was incoherent and reeked of intoxicants. I radioed back to the office that the woman was alive but needed medical attention since she was incapacitated. An ambulance responded to take her to the hospital. It would be the first of many encounters with intoxicated people during my career.

There were also car accidents to deal with late at night. Again, they usually involved a drunk driver who could not navigate the winding park roads while under the influence. Occasionally I would also have to interrupt domestic disputes. One night I heard what sounded like a man striking his wife in a tent as I walked by. I contacted the couple who refused to cooperate with my questions. I made it clear to the man if I heard any more of that during my foot patrols, he would go to jail.

On another busy weekend night, I was patrolling on foot with another college student who was also carrying law enforcement credentials. Approximately 100 yards in front of us we could see in the moonlight a man and a woman grappling with each other on the beach. The man was trying to kiss the woman who was trying to push him away. We stopped to focus our eyes in the darkness to observe what was taking place. The man then tackled the woman and crawled on top of her. We then sprinted to the location and pulled the man off the woman. The man was very intoxicated. The woman was very glad we had come along but refused to press charges since the man was a friend of the family. We made sure the woman got back to the campground safely but could do nothing more.

There were also some strange twists to working at the state park. The park was an inviting place for lovers after dark. The full moon would rise out of Lake Michigan with an unobstructed view for couples snuggling under a blanket at the edge of the sand dunes. If these people were not registered campers, they were supposed to be out of the area by 11pm. Many times couples would be found in the park much later and would be cited as a result. The situations were made more interesting when a half naked Mr. Jones would be found under a blanket with an equally undressed Mrs. Smith. Because the local newspaper would sometimes print the court calendars listing these offenses, the couples had some obvious concerns about their names being listed together. Some of the couples in these liaisons were not real happy that a 20 year old college student was going to hold them accountable for their actions.

Through these diverse kinds of experiences, I became a more experienced officer. As I encountered more complicated situations, I had to learn out of necessity how to adapt and think through these situations on my own. However, I did begin to have doubts the summer I graduated from college, as to whether or not I should stick with law enforcement or take another career path.

I had applied for numerous jobs after graduation with no success. I was struggling with the fact that about half of the jobs were law enforcement positions while the other half were more resource management positions utilizing my land management major. I began to feel that I had to focus on either one or the other, but not both if I was going to get a full-time job.

Late one night I was on my normal foot patrol of the park. The campground was quiet by that time since it was after midnight. I was walking through the picnic area of the park along the lake shore checking for vehicles of any people in the park after curfew hour. There wasn't any sign of anyone outside the campground so I sort of relaxed and instead thought about my career path.

It was a beautiful night with the sky full of stars. I stopped and looked up at the sky and for some reason I thought to myself, "God give me a sign. Should I stay in law enforcement or should I pick another path?" I felt like I was at a fork in the road career-wise. I had to choose one way or the other. In less than two minutes, God answered.

I had barely walked another hundred yards down the road in the dark through the picnic area when I heard two men coming down the slope towards me. I turned on my flashlight and identified myself as a park officer. The men were carrying a half barrel of beer between them. I recognized one of the men as someone who would sometimes sell concessions in the park. However he was not authorized to be in the park after hours. The men set down the heavy half barrel of beer. I informed them that they were in violation of the park curfew. The man I knew then charged me yelling that he was going to break my _____neck!

The man grabbed me by the throat with both hands and began to strangle me. Due to the fact that I had only been taking one week of law enforcement training each summer, I had not yet reached the defensive tactics week. In other words, even though this was my third summer of law enforcement in the park, I had yet to receive any kind of self defense training. Fortunately, I was an athlete in high school and had spent a lot of time lifting weights and running in college. I simply reacted out of instinct and drove my forearm into the man's abdomen, knocking the wind out of him.

The man backed away from me and the two men then disappeared into the brush and the darkness leaving the half barrel of beer behind. I had enough sense not to pursue them by myself while unarmed, so I began a quick hike up to the park office. Just by coincidence, this was the first night that the new park manager was going to be at the park. I had been told he would arrive sometime after dark and would be sleeping on a cot in his office until he found a place to live. I hadn't even met the guy yet and now I was going to the office to wake him up in the dead of night.

I knocked on the closed office door. I heard some movement in the room and a sleepy man opened the door. As the door opened I announced, "Arnie, you don't know me, but it's time to meet the natives." I then explained I had just been assaulted and that I needed some backup to track down the two men. The new park manager quickly got dressed and accompanied me as we went into the park to look for the men. Unfortunately we could not locate them.

The next day we met with the District Attorney in Sheboygan to discuss the case. He typed up charges for the man who had assaulted me. We located the man at his place of work and served him with a complaint. The man eventually paid a $200 fine for disorderly conduct for attempting to strangle a law enforcement officer. The other man was never identified.

In November of that same year the DNR hired me full-time as a Natural Resource Patrol Officer in the Southeast District of Wisconsin. Less than two years later I was promoted to a conservation warden classification. Sometime later after one of those difficult weeks that all officers experience, I thought back to that night in the park when I was assaulted. I remembered how I had asked for a sign. I then thought to myself that I must not be a very good listener because when I received the sign, I had ignored it.

I wondered about my choice at that fork in the road. Eventually, I convinced myself that what the sign really meant was that if I was going to pursue a career in law enforcement; it would include many challenges and difficult times. At least that is what I tried to tell myself because at that point I was committed to sticking with the career. For more than 30 years, the challenges and difficult times would continue.

2 Working in the Hay Barn

My very first day in the field as a conservation warden turned out to be quite eventful. I was assigned to work with the warden in Washington County near West Bend. It was the fall of the year so he intended on giving me some experience checking hunters. However it seemed that fate wanted us to take a different path.

Our first call of the day was a serious automobile accident on a major highway. As would happen many times in my career, we were at the right place at the right time. We were the first law enforcement vehicle to arrive at the scene so we relayed to the dispatchers what emergency response was required as we evaluated injuries.

An hour later we again were diverted from our goal of checking hunters. A deputy had called for assistance in apprehending an escaped prisoner. Once again, we were the closest law enforcement squad in the area. The deputy pointed to a farm in the distance away from his position. He advised us the escapee was last seen running towards that farm.

All three of us drove to the farm. When we arrived, the deputy attempted to make contact in the house while the other warden and I went to the barn. We found the barn door to be locked from the inside. Since I lived on a farm as a boy and had many friends who lived on farms, I knew this was not normal. Farmers don't generally lock their barn doors, especially from the inside. We figured that only the escapee would consider doing that.

A state trooper then arrived on scene to assist. The trooper, the other warden and I then found a way into the barn. After searching the ground floor, we climbed a ladder into the second floor of the barn where the hay was stored. I had been in many hay barns before. In fact as a kid, some of my classmates from school would invite me over to their farm to play games of hide and seek in the hay mow. I never anticipated this would prove to be training for future law enforcement duties.

We did some searching throughout the upper floor of the barn without success. However there was one area of the hay that was fairly steep along one outside wall. Since I was the younger officer, I was volunteered to climb up there to take a look. I figured the escapee had to be up there so I began to make loud comments about getting a pitch fork to stab into the hay. I still got no response.

As I crept along in the dim light looking at the pile of loose hay, I caught a glimpse of a few fingers protruding from the hay. The escapee had literally buried himself in the hay but had failed to completely cover one hand. I yelled down to the other officers that I had a hand up here. The trooper immediately drew his weapon and yelled up to the man to come out with his hands in the air. The escapee didn't move so I pounced on the hay near his exposed hand and grabbed him by the arm. I then pulled him out of the hay and stood the man up so the trooper could see him. When the escapee saw the revolver pointed at him, he decided it was time to surrender.

The other warden thought it was pretty cool that I had apprehended an escapee my first day of work in the field. When I got home that night I called my parents to fill them in on what my first day of work in the field had been like. It was an interesting start to my warden career. However, my parents probably wondered what was coming next.

3 The Death of Jersey Valley Lake

Farming is part of my family history. My great-grandfathers came to America from Germany to farm. Both of my grandfathers owned farms. My father owned a farm while I was a young boy. I understand and appreciate the rural life.

That being said, there are responsible farmers and there are less responsible farmers. When I talk about responsibility, what I refer to is the responsibility to farm in an environmentally sustainable manner. The small family farms of my youth are far less common while the very large corporate style farms are growing in number. Some of these dairy operations milk cows three times a day with round-the-clock workers. These operations produce a lot of milk. They also produce a lot of manure.

Some of the more progressive producers have embraced methane capture and other forms of more environmentally sustainable operations. However, there are others who simply dispose of millions of gallons of liquid manure on the land which is especially challenging in western Wisconsin. The "Driftless Area" of western Wisconsin has steep topography. Farms often occupy the ridge tops and slopes along the top of the ridges. Farm runoff is a concern in these areas because environmentally sensitive trout streams are down slope in the valleys.

After massive fish kills during the 1980's, state environmental laws were created to deal with farm runoff. A chapter of natural resources administrative code called NR243 addresses the issue. Farms that reach a threshold of animal units are required to adhere to nutrient management plans so that the number of animals and the corresponding amount of manure is not too high for the land to absorb. However some farmers intentionally keep their herd a few animals shy of the threshold to avoid the regulations.

The carrying capacity of the land is also a serious concern in western Wisconsin because of what lies beneath the soil surface. This is an area that has what is known as "karst" geology. This is an area with fractured limestone or dolomite as the primary bedrock. These rocks erode underground from water, leading to sinkholes on the land. These fractures and holes in the stone also provide a direct route for surface contaminants to flow rapidly downward into aquifers that feed drinking water wells. If excessive amounts of liquid manure are applied to farm fields, it has to go somewhere. Unfortunately, that can mean groundwater contamination or surface water pollution.

During one spring in Vernon County, there was a heavy snow load on the farm fields well into March. Some farmers rushed to empty their multimillion gallon liquid manure tanks before spring road bans would make their heavy tankers illegal to operate on the roadways. Millions of gallons of liquid manure were applied to the snow on the sloping fields. The ground, still frozen, did not absorb the slushy mix. When warm weather came, rain accompanied the spring warm-up. Adding to the environmental vulnerability of the area was the fact that the Viroqua warden had just retired; meaning there was no warden actively patrolling the part of the county where Jersey Valley Lake is located.

Jersey Valley Lake is a pretty little lake. It is spring fed and also has a pristine stream feeding the lake with clean water. A dam holds back water to a level that allows people to use small row boats and electrically powered craft. Gasoline powered motors are not allowed. Family groups enjoy fishing from the small county park on the south end of the lake. Amish families hike down the hills on the east side of the lake to fish after farm chores are finished. Trout are stocked in the clean waters of the lake by the DNR. The lake also carries a good population of bass and bluegills.

However in this particular spring, all fish life ceased to exist. The rain and warm temperatures melted the snow pack on the farm fields. The melting snow carried with it the toxic slush of manure with it. The large quantity of liquid manure was too much for the land to absorb. Most of it ran down slope into the small stream below. The stream turned from clear to brown as it flowed down its narrow channel to the upper end of the lake.

The lake still encased with a layer of ice, slowly collected the toxic mix under the frozen covering. As the manure began to decompose, the chemical reaction absorbed all of the remaining dissolved oxygen in the water leaving nothing for aquatic life. The fish were all dead in a few short hours.

The first indication of a problem was the odor coming from the lake. Normally the clear lake had no odor. Now it was quite pungent. When the ice melted away, dead game fish washed on to the shore piling up in stinking waves of flesh. By this time, many days had passed since the excessive application of liquid manure. Little evidence remained of the act other than the dead lake below. Wardens from the surrounding area walked the small stream to look for channels of manure or other remaining evidence. The many fingers of ravines extending down to the valley did not pool any manure so the wardens were unable to definitively document which farm had over-applied the manure.

The community was understandably upset that their local lake had been killed. Public meetings with farm groups and legislators were held to discuss the issue. Some called for more rules to stop this from taking place in the future. The sustainable farming movement in the county was especially supportive of change. However the owners of the largest dairy farms were opposed to change. In the end, no new rules resulted.

However the new warden in the county and local county conservation office staff paid closer attention to the area in spring the following years. Local property owners were also more involved in reporting environmental violations which resulted in the prosecution of one farmer for discharging farm waste through buried pipes down slope from his barn. Although not being responsible for this fish kill, the prosecution of the farmer put other farmers in that part of Vernon County on notice that they would also need to be more careful with how they disposed of barn wastes in the future.

The lake eventually began to recover. A fish stocking program was carried out to restock the fish for the future. A costly dam maintenance project was also completed by the county. Today, the lake can once again offer a quality outdoor experience. Hopefully the death of the lake in the past will not be repeated in the future.

Dead fish litter the shore of Jersey Valley Lake

4 Getting Scoped

A game warden faces many dangers. There are risks from Mother Nature in the form of floods, tornadoes, winter storms, and weak ice. There are also vehicle crashes during a pursuit or from collisions with intoxicated drivers. Then there are risks from other humans in the woods. One of the experiences that wardens dread the most is to be scoped.

Getting scoped takes place when a hunter with a rifle points the weapon at the warden as the warden approaches either on foot or in a vehicle. Looking down the barrel of a firearm is not a pleasant feeling. It doesn't matter if the offender is ten feet away with a handgun or 150 yards away with a rifle. The threat is the same, especially during the deer gun season when high powered rifles are used. Rifles used in Wisconsin deer hunting have an effective range of several hundred yards. Therefore if the warden is close enough to see a hunter in a tree stand with his rifle pointed at the warden, the warden is definitely close enough to be shot dead at that same distance.

There are not a lot of reasons why a hunter would point a loaded rifle at another person. The excuse these hunters generally use is that they are simply looking through the scope to identify who is approaching. However the only other alternative that remains is that the hunter is pointing the rifle to make a well-aimed shot that will kill the approaching warden.

I was scoped several times during my career. Early in my career we would usually give the hunter a tongue lashing for their stupidity in pointing a loaded gun at someone. However, a decade later most wardens including myself would seize the firearm and charge the offender with reckless use of a firearm which is a crime in Wisconsin. What prompted us to change how we handled these situations was the death of Warden Andy

Krakow. Andy was shot and killed while sitting in his warden truck in Marquette County. It was not a hunting related incident, but it made us all realize that if someone points a weapon at us as we approach it is prudent to expect the worst of intentions.

In recent years several hunters were given a second chance at life simply because the approaching warden used an extraordinary amount of self control in these situations. There have been wardens in recent years that have been scoped as they approached in full uniform. Yet when the wardens draw their weapon and order the offender to drop the gun, the hunter refuses, forcing the warden to either take a life or to continue to scream at the hunter to drop the gun. This extra amount of time looking down the barrel of a rifle puts the warden in significant danger in a life or death situation because the hunter is now adding a new element to the situation.

At this point, the hunter has already identified who is approaching. Yet the hunter still refuses to lower the weapon. It is an unfortunate escalation of aggression in the outdoors that is becoming increasingly common. Some of this aggression is also being directed at other hunters.

During my last decade as a warden, I noticed a troubling trend. The week before the deer season, people would stop in to the DNR office to talk with me. They all had something in common. They enjoyed deer hunting but were concerned about opening weekend of the deer season as it was approaching. They were concerned because they felt that they had a neighbor who was crazy to the point of being dangerous. These people would share past stories of armed aggression by a neighboring property owner.

Some of these hostile men would call them on the phone to tell the neighbors that if he saw them cross the property line during the deer season, they would be shot. Others were a bit less direct and would simply post signs on the fence line that trespassers would be shot. In a few cases, the crazy neighbors would actually fire rounds over people if they got close to the fence even though they were still on their own land. I found it incredibly disheartening that a District Attorney in one county refused to prosecute the offender for these actions. All of these complaints came in the years before six hunters were killed in a hunter confrontation in Sawyer County in 2004.

Fortunately there has been a trend in other counties to take these violations more seriously. After all, some of these perceived indiscretions during the deer season are accidental. One young boy in his teens became lost during a deer hunt in LaCrosse County and wandered off in the wrong direction. When he saw a residence he walked towards it to ask for help to find his way home. The landowner saw the young hunter on his property and responded by stepping out on his back deck and firing rifle shots over the boy's head. The man then pointed the rifle at the boy and ordered the boy to surrender his weapon. The property owner was prosecuted and convicted in LaCrosse County. One can only hope that all prosecutors in Wisconsin will take the position that none of this aggression in the outdoors should be tolerated.

5 An Appreciation for Bluegills

I have a true appreciation for bluegills. Other anglers may consider them to be too humble a fish. After all, they don't even reach a foot in length. The tournament crowd may scoff and state that people don't enter national bluegill contests. In a way I think that is a good thing.

Many Wisconsin anglers owe their initial love of the sport of fishing to a day in their past when they caught their first feisty bluegill. The fish was eager to bite a piece of worm and make a run for it; causing the red and white bobber to dance on the water surface above. I have yet to see a small child who wasn't happy to catch their first bluegill.

That is why I always shook my head at the lack of respect some ice fishermen showed to these important fish. It was common during my winter patrols to see dozens of small bluegills dead on the ice around abandoned ice holes. The anglers apparently didn't like the fact that the smaller bluegills were grabbing their baits before larger ones could strike. The angler would respond by throwing the small fish on the ice to die. What a waste I thought. You don't grow 9 inch bluegills by killing 6 inch bluegills. That is the problem with some outdoor users. They don't care about tomorrow's resources. They only care about what they can take home today.

During my career there were a number of occasions when I would fish undercover to observe other ice fishermen when the bluegills were biting. A few learned the hard way that when they threw bluegills on to the ice to die, those fish were considered part of their daily bag limit. They may have stopped at 25 fish in their bucket but when adding in a dozen left dead on the ice, they were definitely over their bag limit.

When it comes to the best tasting fish, it is hard to beat fresh bluegill fillets fried in butter with just a bit of light seasoning on top. There are other people who also like to eat bluegills. Sometimes those people forget there is a thing called a daily bag limit.

There was a man well-known to wardens in the LaCrosse area who also loved to eat bluegills. He loved to eat them so much that he was often taking home more than his fair share. During the most recent incident when the man was cited, I was on Lake Onalaska with another warden working a complaint that the man was again taking too many fish. We had an idea where to look for him so we put our boat on the water early in the morning to wait for his arrival. We later found him fishing south of the three man-made islands in the middle of the lake. From almost a quarter mile away, we watched the man fish with our binoculars with the sun at our back. We could see him catching bluegill after bluegill from the shallow water along the island. We saw him keep more than his daily limit of 25 fish and he was still fishing.

We discussed our options. We could rush him with our boat to try to get to him with the evidence or we could wait until he went in to shore to unload his catch at his lakeside home. We went with the second option since it is too easy for a fish poacher to toss his bucket of illegal fish over the side when the warden approaches. The man was retired and walked slowly with a heavy build so we anticipated we could catch up to him before he got from his pier to his home. That is exactly the way the situation played out. After the man pulled anchor, we shadowed his boat until he had tied up his boat at this pier. When he stepped from the boat with the fish, we rushed in with our boat. I leaped from the boat as he reached the halfway point to his garage. I sprinted up the hill and caught up to him as he opened his garage door. After displaying my warden credentials, I asked for the bucket of fish.

The man knew the drill. This was in fact the fourth or fifth time in 20 years that he was going to be cited for taking more than his bag limit of bluegills in the LaCrosse area. We seized all of the fish as evidence and issued the citation.

We talked to the man for a while in his home. The home was filled with fish and game mounts from all over the world. The man was what we call a harvester. He had spent his entire life in pursuit of fish and game. That in itself was fine. However he believed that limits were for other people, not for him.

We struggled with the local court system over license revocations for the man. He had been revoked before for his fishing violations only to have his attorney lobby a local judge to reduce the length of the revocation. His only real defense was that he couldn't count to 25 when the fish were biting. The last time he was in court, the warden acting as the court officer reminded the man to carry a clicker to click each time he kept a fish so he didn't need to keep track of the number of fish in his head. The man still fishes local waters and I suspect he still keeps too many fish if given the opportunity.

Some anglers who also appreciate the humble bluegill will try just about anything to take some home. During a training assignment in Madison during my first year as a warden, I saw something that I couldn't quite believe. I was on patrol with my training officer in the city of Madison when we stopped a short distance away from Lake Monona. A man was hunkered down along a storm sewer grate at the edge of a busy street. We stopped because the man had an ice fishing jig pole in his hands. This obviously didn't look normal since the edge of the lake was 50 feet away.

As we approached the man he pulled a bluegill up through the storm drain grate! We both looked at each other in disbelief before contacting the man. After identifying ourselves as conservation wardens we asked the man what he was doing. He told us that there was a warm water discharge that flowed beneath the storm sewer grate into the lake. Just by chance he found that bluegills came up the warm water discharge from the lake to look for food. He was more than happy to provide bait to them.

While we were talking to him, he pulled another bluegill up through the gap between the metal grates. He pointed out to us that his unique technique only worked on bluegills and crappies due to their flat body structure. If he hooked a bass or perch they could not be caught because their bodies were wider than the gaps in the storm sewer grate. This fishing technique gave new meaning to the term "slot size limit."

6 System Failures

You cannot work within state government for very long without recognizing that it is an imperfect system. Due to changes in state law under Governor Tommy Thompson's administration, DNR leadership is now politically appointed rather than being selected by the Natural Resources Board based on qualifications and experience. A political appointee is given the DNR Secretary position, the highest job in the DNR, with multiple layers below the Secretary position also being filled by political appointees.

These appointees can be selected strictly for political reasons. Some top appointees do not have a college degree or any kind of natural resource related experience. In this system, the top fifty percent of the DNR supervisory chain of command is removed and replaced by political appointees on average every four years. When people complain about how the DNR is run, I always tell them, "Name me one successful private company that removes and replaces the top fifty percent of its leadership team every four years." I have yet to meet anyone who can name a single company. Yet that is how our state agencies are run.

In this political work environment, "the message" from DNR headquarters is tightly controlled. In recent years, DNR employees who were best qualified to testify at legislative hearings on proposed law changes were not allowed to do so. This is especially true if the proposed legislation may not be in the best interest of our natural resources. There have been a surprising number of natural resource related legislative bills in recent years on which the DNR has taken no position. DNR employees definitely had a position on the legislation. However, they were ordered not to testify against the bills.

Under such a system, creativity and risk taking is often subtly discouraged. Political appointees want their agency to maintain a low profile while they are in charge. The reason is because they know that with a new election in four years, they may need to land in another bureaucratic job in another agency to stay employed. Drawing attention to one's self with a few agency blunders could result in no job offers in state government after the next election.

This reluctance to take risks or to challenge the status quo in an agency can be very frustrating for people working at the field level. Employees who are the most innovative and forward thinking often hit consistent roadblocks. Workers in the outdoors who want to improve the system are sometimes looked at as rebels or loose cannons. Yet out of dedication, some people still try to create change.

I found myself in such as situation as I ended my years as a field warden in the late 1980's. During thousands of fishing license checks it became painfully obvious to me that there was a significant problem with a state law that granted permanent free fishing licenses to people for a variety of reasons. I totally agree that individuals with special needs should be given special opportunities to enjoy the outdoors in order to overcome adversity. However, after seeing literally hundreds of special licenses in a year's time, one incident finally made me say enough is enough. This took place when I checked a fisherman who was carrying a very heavy cooler filled with ice and beer.

When I asked to see the man's fishing license he showed me a free lifetime disabled fishing license. In my eyes he definitely did not look disabled since he was a young man in his late 20's. He was also carrying a cooler up a steep river bank that probably weighed 80 pounds. I noted that the man had been issued the license 8 years earlier.

When I politely asked him why he had the license, he said he had burned his back at work that year. It didn't require a medical degree to know that a burn isn't going to take 8 years to heal. Yet the man still had a free lifetime fishing license. On other occasions I had found people with free lifetime licenses because they said they had high blood pressure. I thought about all the wardens doing their job with high blood pressure yet they did not carry free lifetime fishing licenses.

When I was promoted to LaCrosse to be the warden supervisor there, I also noticed people were being issued free lifetime fishing licenses for another reason. I began to have encounters with people who advised they were being issued the free lifetime licenses when they were patients at drug and alcohol treatment institutions. The state law for the free lifetime licenses at that time specified that people with disabilities or who were "institutionalized" qualified for free lifetime fishing licenses. In other words, people arrested for operating a motor vehicle while intoxicated were now receiving free fishing licenses for life for being a drunk driver! To say that this frustrated me was an understatement.

I was able to convince the Bureau of Law Enforcement to provide me with funding to hire a part-time employee for one summer who would conduct surveys of the outlets for these free lifetime fishing licenses. I knew I wasn't going to get anywhere trying to change the problem without documentation. I also requested other wardens from around the state to share information with me on any problems they were having with permanent free licenses in their area.

When the survey was completed we verified that alcohol

treatment centers were issuing the free fishing licenses to drunk drivers receiving treatment at their centers. The facilities usually stated they told the people to turn in the licenses at the end of their treatment but hardly anyone did. We also focused on the "disabled' part of the problem clarifying what various forms of social security assistance should and should not be accepted for a disabled fishing license.

I contacted the head of the DNR licensing division and asked him to estimate how many free permanent disabled fishing licenses he felt were in circulation. He estimated it could be as high as 50,000 licenses. He also added that for these licenses the state did not receive the annual $5 grant in federal funds for each license sold because these were free licenses. In other words just for the loss of federal funds alone we were losing $250,000 a year in revenue for conservation programs without counting the additional loss of fishing license revenue if the license had been sold.

Fortunately, this kind of financial hit to the agency was a problem that everyone felt should be addressed when my report was circulated. The legislature then changed their law to tighten up the entire issue. Today, there is a reduced fee annual disabled fishing license that is available for qualified individuals. Because it is an annual license, people who heal up from injuries no longer get a permanent license for a temporary injury. Likewise, drunk drivers are no longer issued free fishing licenses. It all seems like common sense, but unfortunately common sense is not always rewarded. Throughout my career I worked with other wardens and department staff on many similar issues. I submitted dozens of proposals that were never acted upon, usually without any feedback as to why. Some of the proposals I had to submit multiple times because the political appointees in the Secretary's office "lost" them.

Just one example of another proposal I submitted that was permanently lost without explanation was a law change to prohibit the possession of alligators, crocodiles and deadly foreign snakes by private citizens in Wisconsin. Each year a wide variety of foreign animals and reptiles make their way into Wisconsin. Every year someone finds an alligator in the Mississippi River released by someone who didn't want to feed it anymore. Piranha and other exotic fish are also found.

This concern involves drug dealers who order deadly venomous snakes over the internet. The snake crate is delivered by UPS to the citizen's front door. The snake is used as a home security system for drug dealers concerned that someone may enter the home to steal their drugs. If the venomous snake escapes from the home, other local residents and children could be at great risk. Do we really need to allow local residents to possess a King Cobra or Pit Viper in homes in our neighborhoods? Some counties are now enacting county ordinances to deal with deadly pets. However it would make sense to do this as a statewide rule for consistency purposes.

I also submitted a request for a law change to create a civil forfeiture for careless use of a firearm while hunting. During the course of hunting accident investigations, there have been many examples of hunters who were doing really stupid things with their weapons. Some of these situations result in wounded people or bullet holes in homes. Yet some of the people responsible for these situations were never charged due to the reluctance of prosecutors to charge the offender with a crime.

A couple of District Attorneys have advised me during my career that the reckless use of a firearm charge does not always fit these situations. They feel that this particular charge requires evidence that the person with the gun intentionally pointed the weapon at a person. However there are many other careless acts causing injury or property damage that do not fall under that law. For example I watched a pheasant hunter in Jefferson County shoot a shotgun at a pheasant he flushed from the grass. The problem is that he did so as he walked back to the parking lot at a public hunting ground. The bird flew low in line with parked cars but the man shot anyway; rattling shot off other hunters' cars and causing other people including myself to take cover. No charges were filed because the man was intentionally pointing the weapon at a bird not at people. The parking lot was simply in the background. This is an example of a careless act that could be addressed with a citation instead of a criminal complaint.

Similar situations develop when a man with a rifle fires multiple shots at a deer running across an open field with homes in the background. Some District Attorneys will charge the man for reckless use of a firearm while others will not. If a hunter accidently discharges his weapon into the body of a companion or another hunter nearby, should they not be held accountable for the careless handling of the weapon? How can a turkey hunter not be convicted for shooting at movement when the movement turns out to be a person?

Most people would also be surprised to know that there is no "implied consent" law for hunters with firearms. If a person is driving a boat, snowmobile, or ATV, the law requires them to submit to a preliminary breath test if a law enforcement officer has reason to believe they are intoxicated. However this law does not apply to a hunter armed with a deadly weapon. Therefore, wardens have a more difficult time enforcing the intoxicated possession of a firearm law. Common sense would suggest that the state legislature would want to make sure that intoxicated hunters are removed from the woods. However, not having an "implied consent" law that applies to hunters or other armed individuals in possession of a firearm conflicts with that assumption.

One of the reasons these proposals die is because of the almost total absence of bi-partisanship in the State Legislature. Since the DNR Secretary is now a political appointee, any bill coming out of the DNR is now viewed as a bill that is coming from the Governor's office. If there is a Democratic Governor, the Republican controlled Assembly opposes all DNR statutory requests. The opposing political party does not support DNR bills because that is considered to be an act of support for the Governor.

This is a very unfortunate situation. There are many laws that need to be updated, fixed, or eliminated that have an impact on the natural resources of our state or affect the safety of outdoor users. When a major state newspaper reports that several thousand convicted felons purchase deer gun licenses each year, legislators tell reporters that the DNR isn't doing its job. However, only the legislature has the authority to change state statutes to make it illegal for felons to purchase firearm licenses.

Unfortunately, there isn't much hope these examples of poor laws will be changed soon. For that to be possible, the Secretary of the DNR must be selected by a citizen board. In the past this was done through a competitive application process evaluating multiple candidates based on their experience and qualifications. Contrast that to the current procedure where the Governor appoints someone to repay a political favor.

7 How About Those Packers?

During my first deer season as a conservation warden, I was assigned to work in Sheboygan County. My parents lived in the county so the Department could save on lodging expenses during my assignment if I stayed at my parent's home. In the early 1980's, deer season work generally meant working from before dawn to late at night. The number of complaints received during those seasons, far exceeded the number received during deer seasons in recent years.

The second day of the season the warden assigned to the county received a radio call from the Sheriff's Department dispatcher. The dispatcher advised that there was a man at a tavern near the Parnell tower who wanted to meet with a warden to talk about an illegal deer. The dispatcher was sharp enough to note that the man was intoxicated and sounded like he was going to be trouble so she recommended that the warden not go alone. I was the second warden to respond.

We arrived at the bar together and walked inside. It was Sunday, the second day of the deer season. About 8 men were seated at the bar when we walked in. The complainant was already standing inside the door waiting for us. After the other warden introduced himself, the complainant grabbed him by his uniform jacket, pushed him up against the wall, and the two of them then tumbled down the front steps out the front door of the bar.

Now I had only been a warden for three weeks at that time. I was totally shocked that my partner was now wrestling outside the front door with this intoxicated man. However my attention out of necessity had to instead focus on the other 8 men seated at the bar. I knew I had to keep the situation from getting worse.

I couldn't let those 8 additional men join the fight with my partner.

My fears began to be realized as the men set down their glasses of beer and rose from their bar stools to join the fight outside. What was I going to do now? In those days we didn't have Tasers, or collapsible batons, or even pepper spray. We had our bare hands and a revolver and nothing else in between. I considered going to the opposite side of the pool table in the bar room to pick up a pool cue to try to control the mob. But somehow that didn't sound like an idea that would work either.

Then, as the men stood up to leave their bar stools to walk towards me, I glanced above them at the television screen above the bar. Because the Sunday Packer game was about to begin, an interview about the Packer game had just begun on the television. I pointed at the television screen and yelled "How about those Packers? Do you think we are going to win today?"

Fortunately, one of the men took the bait. He said, "Ya hey, I think them Packers got a good chance." The man then eased back on to his bar stool and picked up his beer as he began to talk about the game. The other men stopped and first looked outside towards the front door before sitting down at the bar to pick up their glasses of beer. I kept the conversation going about the Packer game and a few minutes later the complainant and other warden came back into the bar.

The other warden was able to calm the angry man down and diffused the situation. Ironically, the man wasn't calling about an illegal deer at all. A neighbor near the bar was butchering a pig and the complainant in his intoxicated state, wanted to see if the warden could tell the difference between a pig carcass and a deer carcass. The warden used a lot of discretion and decided not to charge the man for the altercation. Meanwhile, I left

feeling very lucky that deer hunters in Wisconsin are good
Packer fans.

8 Embracing the Darkness

Game wardens spend an entire career doing their best to blend in to natural surroundings in the outdoors. There are numerous kinds of violations that need to be witnessed in person for the warden to take the appropriate action. A warden who simply conducts boat landing checks isn't going to do much good in the duck marsh. A good warden recognizes that direct observation is an important tool in an effective enforcement program.

During daylight hours, wardens try to hide in plain sight using camouflage clothes. Wardens learn the importance of breaking up the outline of their body by hiding behind brush or a tree. A tree also provides a shield for errant steel shot flying through the air over a duck marsh. At other times in a duck marsh, a warden may spend several hours standing in a patch of willows behind a firing line to observe hunters who may be taking more than their daily bag limit of canvasbacks.

Having the ability to disappear during daylight hours allowed me to apprehend a man shooting at a tundra swan on Lake Onalaska. I saw the swan approaching from several hundred yards away. I didn't expect anyone to shoot at the swan since the majority of hunters can identify the large birds. However on this day, a man 75 yards away from me swung on the bird with his shotgun and fired. Steel shot struck the underside of the swan's wings. The bird shuddered a bit in flight but continued flying. I wondered if the bird would succumb to its injuries later. I pulled my small boat from its hiding place in the tall wild rice bed and went to the man to make contact. I informed him he would be receiving a citation for shooting at a bird during the closed season. He was surprised that a warden had been observing the action from a location so close to him.

On another day I was standing in a cornfield in Jefferson County. Two waterfowl hunters were shooting at mallards flying into the already harvested part of the field in front of me. The mallards were there to gobble down corn kernels that had escaped the combine. One of the hunters shot a mallard that dropped hard to the ground to the right of my position. I was surprised that the hunter would carry the mallard past me just two corn rows away without even noticing I was there.

Being able to covertly observe duck hunters in the early 1980's was important for wardens due to a unique bag limit structure in place at the time called the point system. Under this law, waterfowl hunters had to follow a bag limit based on how many points of ducks they shot each day. Not only did the law specify how many birds could be shot each day, it also specified what order ducks could be shot in.

For example on opening day in the 1983 season, hen mallards were worth 100 points and a hunter could only shoot ducks until he met or exceeded 100 points with the last bird. Meanwhile blue-winged teal were only worth 10 points. So theoretically, a hunter could shoot 9 teal before ending the day with a hen mallard. On the other hand, if the hunter shot a hen mallard first, he was done for the day.

Hunters tried various ways to get around this such as by gutting some ducks as soon as they were shot to "cool them down." This was done to prepare for a possible encounter with a warden who would use a rectal thermometer to take a body temperature of the ducks to see which ducks were shot last. Other hunters would decapitate any hen mallard they shot to claim the duck was actually a drake mallard worth only 35 points. These hunters would unfortunately discover they had earned themselves a citation by not knowing in advance that wardens were trained to confirm the sex of mallards by a subtle difference in the coloring of the wing.   Overall the point system was a complicated law that wardens were happy to see eliminated.

There are other reasons why it is important to be able to covertly observe hunters. Some hunters intentionally waste our natural resources. Several times I observed duck hunters to leave ducks in the marsh rather than take them home. In one case a man was shooting ducks in the dim light as the hunting hours began. He was dropping ducks including a coot that he misidentified in flight. The coot was left when he went back to the boat landing. On another lake I watched a duck hunter to shoot and retrieve a duck. When he saw that he had shot a merganser, a less tasty fish eating duck, he held the duck in his hand like a football and threw the duck away into the tall marsh grass behind him.

On other occasions other wardens and I have watched duck hunters to drop multiple ducks without making any effort to retrieve them. Some hunters apparently only enjoy the shooting part of the hunt. These hunters or I should say shooters; choose to make little effort to retrieve the birds they kill because that would bring them to their daily bag limit quicker. These are people who don't want a limit of ducks to take home. They simply want to shoot more.

During snowier deer gun seasons, wardens use deer decoys to apprehend poachers shooting deer from the highway. A warden on foot has to find a way to hide in these conditions so they can document the violation. The warden in hiding also has to radio other wardens in the chase car down the road to advise which vehicle needs to be stopped. To hide in these conditions as well as to be visible when they need to be, wardens spread a white sheet over them as they stretch out on the ground in a sleeping bag to stay warm. Then if a poacher shoots at the decoy or tries to walk out to it, the warden can climb out from the sleeping bag with their blaze orange uniform on to make contact with the hunter.

Sometimes hunters are oblivious to the presence of a warden when we are seated in our unmarked warden trucks. During the deer gun season in Vernon County I was parked in a hunter parking lot adjacent to the Rush Creek Wildlife area. I was trying to covertly observe a hunter returning to a vehicle some distance away that had dropped a pop can on the ground when he left the vehicle to enter the woods to hunt. While waiting for him to return, another group of three hunters returned to a different vehicle parked just to my right. The people looked around to see if anyone was in the area before pulling out a bag of marijuana to roll some marijuana cigarettes. Naturally they were surprised when I appeared at the driver's side window as the driver inhaled deeply on the marijuana cigarette.

Undercover techniques also work well on ice fishermen. In Jefferson County, I had been a warden for more than 5 years when I was finally issued a truck instead of a squad car. Having a truck with higher ground clearance allowed me to patrol Lake Koshkonong on the ice with a vehicle for the first time. To look like other ice fishermen, I put a blaze orange shell over my warden coat and placed a bucket with tip-ups in the back of the truck so that people could see the orange flags from the tip-ups blowing in the wind. From a distance I looked like any other fishermen. The first month I used the truck on the ice, I issued more than 30 citations to ice fishermen, usually for using more than their legal number of lines. They were very surprised to see me in a vehicle that was capable of being driven around the lake.

However for some investigations, wardens must wait for darkness in order to do their work. People who are afraid of the dark cannot survive in a game warden job. Wardens embrace the darkness because it allows them to reach areas undetected that would not be accessible in daylight hours. Working at night in a state park during the summers I was in college allowed me to learn how invisible an officer in the dark can be to the average person.

On several occasions I would be on foot patrol in the park watching for juvenile drinking parties or illegal damage to trees or facilities. Young people drinking beer around campfires would need to walk through the campground to reach the restrooms on a regular basis. Sometimes these young drinkers would decide it was too far to walk. Several times as I walked past campsites, a young woman would leave the bright firelight and walk into the darkness to the edge of the park road. The woman would then stop to urinate rather than walk all the way to the restroom. In about the same amount of time it took to finish the job, the young woman's eyesight would adjust to the darkness. Then she would realize she had stopped to urinate right in front of a lawman. The woman would then quickly pull up her pants and run back to the campfire.

While working deer shiners, we would sometimes see other violations taking place. I was in my truck with another warden on the bluff above the city of LaCrosse watching for deer shiners. It was an area where we were getting complaints of deer poaching by a group of archers who were targeting large bucks around the perimeter of the city. We had parked behind some construction equipment where the weather service office now stands. When we saw a vehicle approaching at a very slow speed we waited in anticipation for a spotlight to be used.

However the headlights were turned off and the vehicle pulled to a stop less than 50 feet away from us. When the dome light came on inside the vehicle, we observed the occupants snorting cocaine. They were very surprised to see us when we appeared at both windows. Deer poaching work then had to be placed on hold while we transported the people downtown to the police department with the evidence.

Some locations of illegal activity dictated that a warden could only approach under cover of darkness. If a deer hunter was hunting over an illegal bait pile where he had a long range view of the surrounding area, the investigating warden would sometimes choose to enter the area under cover of darkness before dawn. The warden would already be on location when the hunter arrived later.

If the warden is checking raccoon hunters, the action is all taking place at night. Some coon hunters have been known to poach a buck with a 22 caliber rifle at night during the rut. With information from a reliable complainant, the warden may be hidden in the woods far from the road, waiting to see if the coon hunters will stop on a farm lane to shine a remote picked cornfield for deer.

I had one unique experience walking in the dark to observe what a coon hunter was doing. This was at a time when wardens were trying to address a large amount of illegal raccoon shining that was taking place due to high fur prices. Many people were simply walking around at night with a spotlight to shine coon which was illegal. I was following a man working a spotlight in front of me on foot. I was attempting to circle around him through a pasture area when I stopped near a woodpile in front of me to look at the man through my binoculars. When I put the binoculars down, I noticed the woodpile was moving! I didn't want to turn my flashlight on to give away my position but I definitely wanted to know what was moving around in front of me. I began to think pasture, cow pasture, or was this a breeding bull in front of me? Fortunately for me it turned out to be a harmless Holstein cow. I was also able to gather enough evidence to cite the man for shining wild animals.

This was also a year when people were using small motorboats to shine raccoon from. Shining wild animals while in possession of a firearm is just as illegal from a boat as it is from shining with a gun from a car. During one fall, we apprehended three different groups of "boat shiners" in Jefferson County. The last one was unique because we had the DNR airplane in the air that night. The pilot directed my squad in on the suspects as they were navigating back on a small river to their vehicle parked near a highway bridge. Because it was also the end of the 4 hour enforcement flight for the pilot, the other three warden squads decided to drive to our location to see if they could help out. When the coon shiners pulled their flat bottom boat up on shore in front of their van, 8 game wardens stepped out from behind the van to greet them. I imagine the coon shiners will never forget that moment.

During spring walleye spawning time, I spent many hours on northern lakes in remote areas, watching to see if someone would walk in to the lake to shine and spear walleyes in the middle of the night. During one of those nights I discovered I was not alone. I had been dropped off on a lake by the local warden in northern Wisconsin who instructed me to observe the lake from a very narrow point of land that extended in to the main part of the lake. It was after midnight when I heard loud crunching and crashing 50 yards behind me. I soon figured out that a bear, hungry from winter hibernation, was pulling apart half rotted logs nearby. He was apparently looking for grubs or insects to eat. My only way out was on a narrow path past the bear. I had no problem staying awake on my lake surveillance that night.

There are some lighter moments that come with working in the darkness. One night I was seated in my squad car with a deputy who also worked for our agency as a part-time warden. It was Halloween night. I always made a point of working shiners on

43

Halloween because it never seemed to be a dull night when I did. On this particular night we were backed into the woods on an almost invisible forest trail along a thickly forested road. We heard a car coming down the road at a high rate of speed. The car screeched to a stop almost in front of us. We then heard empty aluminum cans to be thrown from the vehicle striking trees and landing on the road in multiple directions.

After stopping for a few moments to relieve themselves on the road, several of the occupants began running up and down the road screaming. They apparently were fans of the popular horror flick called, "Halloween" in which a guy named Jason goes around town wearing a hockey mask killing people. Several kids were running up and down the road yelling, "Jason, Jason, come out and get us Jason!" One young man stopped on the road directly in front of us as he called out to Jason. I looked at the deputy and smiled and simply said, "Should we?"

The deputy laughed as he read my mind and said, "Sure, we already have a littering violation." With that vote of support I fired up the engine and began driving forward out of the darkness towards the young man. I would imagine his eyes must have been as big as saucers. For a brief moment he probably thought someone with a hockey mask was in the approaching vehicle. Kids raced to get back into the car. We turned on our red light and headlights and pulled in front of the vehicle. A half dozen shaking teenagers were inside. I let the deputy deal with the underage drinking while I addressed the littering of the cans along the road.

Although this previous experience was quite funny, there is a very real element of danger conducting law enforcement at night. Sometimes wardens respond to a scene of a violation without knowing how many individuals are involved, how many suspects may be in the woods hiding with a gun, or how many of the suspects have serious criminal records.

During one of my last deer seasons, I was working with Shawna in Vernon County. She asked me to assist in investigating a complaint of a group of deer hunters who had basically bullied their way on to a property owned by an elderly widow. They had made neighboring property owners nervous because they knew one member of the hunting group was a convicted felon. The widow was too intimidated by the group to tell them they couldn't hunt on her land. Shawna also advised there was an active arrest warrant out for the felon.

We found vehicles on the woman's land an hour before dark. We parked a half a mile away so that the felon would not see us as he left the woods. We didn't want him to hide his weapon on the way out of the woods which would void the possession of a firearm by a felon violation. We observed an older man and woman riding out of the woods on an ATV with uncased rifles. We figured those two people were the felon's parents based on the information we had. Although the uncased weapon on an ATV was a violation under the law at that time, we chose to wait for the felon since that was the more serious offense.

As it got increasingly dark, the gathering darkness reached the point where we could no longer observe what was taking place around the small travel trailer the group used as their camp. I then decided to approach the camp on foot so that I could relay what was taking place on my portable radio to Shawna in the warden truck. I wanted her to remain there so we could make sure we had radio communication with the Sheriff's department in this hilly terrain. When dealing with felons, you always want to be able to call for backup officers if needed. After I looked both ways for approaching headlights, I jogged down the road in the dark to reach the camp. As the night closed in around me, I quietly slid down the road embankment to hide beneath the ATV trailer. The first two hunters we saw were seated in the van only a few feet away. They had no idea I was there. A few minutes later, I observed a vehicle approaching from the opposite direction.

After the car was parked, the felon and his hunting companion each stepped out of the car with a cased firearm. After they put the guns in the trailer and stepped back outside I made contact with the men while they were unarmed. I then radioed Shawna to come down to the camp. I started the contact as if it was a routine license check. Shawna parked her truck facing the trailer. I told the men to turn around with their backs to the truck headlights so we could read the information on their back tags. I then pointed at the felon's back to Shawna who knew I had found the felon. She had handcuffs on the man before anyone knew what was happening. It was a successful case of embracing the darkness in order to arrest a serious criminal without incident.

9 Undercover in Two Rivers

I was a recruit warden on my third training assignment in 1982. Recruit wardens usually spend their first year moving around the state, changing training officers every six to eight weeks. This gives the inexperienced wardens a flavor for how the job is different depending on which part of the state they get stationed in. Being a game warden in Racine is much different that being the game warden in Rhinelander.

In this assignment I was stationed in Sturgeon Bay. While visiting the regional office with my training officer one day, we were told that there was a complaint of a man who had been catching and selling trout and salmon in Two Rivers in Manitowoc County. This was illegal because game fish caught by hook and line cannot be sold. Only rough fish like carp or commercial fish taken by a commercial licensee can be sold when taken from the wild.

Wisconsin has a special investigation unit of wardens who work on the illegal commercialization of our natural resources. However due to the small number of officers in the unit, they usually focus on much larger cases than a single man selling some fish out of his home. Knowing those limitations, the warden supervisor at the regional office asked if I would be interested in trying to purchase some fish from the man. The logic was that I was a new face that nobody would recognize. I was also quite young looking at the time so it was believed the man would not be as quick to suspect me.

I was aware that as a recruit it is seldom a good idea to say no to an offer of another work assignment so I agreed to volunteer. Another warden gave me the man's phone number and told me to come up with a story that the man would believe and to make the call. I thought about the situation for a few minutes and sat down at a desk at the DNR office and made the phone call to the suspect. Obviously this was in the days before caller ID.

When the man answered I told him I had been fishing on the piers in Lake Michigan and had not had any success. I was trying to get a few trout for a bachelor's party of one of my friends. I told him another fisherman had told me the man was a very good fisherman and might be able to help me out. The suspect's ego got the best of him. He began to talk about how he was one of the best fishermen in the area and that he uses techniques that no one else knows about. He agreed to meet with me at this house.

Because I was traveling to my training assignments in a squad car, I obviously could not use that vehicle to make the undercover buy. The wardens instead obtained the personal truck of a local warden who met me outside the DNR office an hour before the meeting time. The truck was running when I got in so off I went. I found the house alright, turned off the truck, and put the ring of keys in my pocket.

I wore a pair of blue jeans and a college t-shirt that I had with me for my days off. I had only been out of college a few years so when I met the fisherman I told him I was a college drop-out at UW-Green Bay and that I worked on campus on grounds maintenance mowing lawns. The man seemed to believe the story. He told me to come in the house.

As I entered the home, we walked down the stairs into the basement. Another man was waiting in a side room next to a large freezer. The man didn't say anything, he just stared at me. I then began to think about what I had got myself into. I had not brought along anything with me that would suggest I was a warden. I had no badge, no gun, and no means of self-defense. I also had no phone or radio to call for help. There were no back-up officers down the street. I suddenly felt very alone.

The fisherman opened the freezer and help up a variety of frozen trout and salmon. I was nervous but decided to play the game slow so I passed the time for a while talking about how to catch fish from the piers. The fisherman was all too willing to brag about how he did so. Eventually he asked me if I would pay $20 for each large fish. I didn't have enough cash for both at that price so the suspect agreed to subtract a few dollars off the total price. Then the other guy took a step or two towards me and asked if I was a game warden. I did my best to act like that was a ridiculous idea. The other man then made it clear that if I was, bad things were going to happen. I wondered how many hours or days it would take for someone to find my remains if that happened. I wished there was another warden waiting down the street to back me up, but that wasn't the case. I tried to focus on the task at hand and simply pulled out the cash from my pocket and paid the fisherman.

The fisherman and I then walked back out of the house with the fish to the truck. After putting the fish in the back of the truck, I climbed into the driver's seat with the fisherman at my truck window. The man was quite talkative by this time. He bragged that he was the talk of the town in recent weeks because of the way he was killing the fish. He said that some people were getting mad at him because of all of the fish he was keeping. He then added, "When I go fishing I don't go for two or three fish. I go for my limit, or more, or more...." He was laughing as he said, "or more, or more." I let the man talk as I pulled the very large ring of keys from my pocket. I looked at the keys and saw all kinds of ignition keys on the ring. I didn't know which one to use!

The man continued to talk and I tried to act interested as I tried key after key with my right hand, trying to do so in a manner that the fisherman would not notice. I was trying to push key after key into the ignition by feel so he could not see that I was having a problem with the ring of keys. When a key finally went in and the engine fired I was never so relieved in my whole life. I said goodbye to the man and drove back to the DNR office in Green Bay.

When I got there I tagged the fish with evidence tags and began to write an incident report. I was seated at my desk writing the report when my trainer warden arrived and asked what happened. I told him I had successfully purchased two trout from the suspect. My trainer warden, not known for a lot of positive feedback said, "He must have been really dumb," and walked away. A week later, I was asked to make another purchase from the man to establish a pattern of illegal sales.

The second purchase was a lot easier. I made a note of which key was the appropriate ignition key for the truck before I got out the second time. The man's friend was also absent which was a big relief. Before the fisherman showed me the fish he was going to sell, he asked me to smoke some marijuana. I declined and told him I had smoked too much in college and had decided I wasn't going to smoke anymore. He accepted the response. After I bought two more fish, we started to talk about deer hunting. He asked me about hunting on some public lands in the area. I told him I stayed away from there because of the hunting pressure.

It was odd, but that simple phrase hunting pressure made the man uneasy. I guess it sounded too much like a DNR term. He seemed to be a little uneasy after I said it. Since I had already paid for the fish, I made an excuse to leave and took the fish with me. I put the right key in the ignition and left shortly after.

Several weeks later the man was served with a criminal complaint for the illegal sale of game fish. He apparently made a guilty plea in court because I never had to return to testify at a trial. I never pursued any positions with the special investigative unit after that. As far as I was concerned I already had enough of working undercover.

10 Long Day on the Bark River

My first waterfowl season as a warden assigned to Jefferson County took place in 1982. Since I had only been in the county for a week before the duck season, my supervisor paired me up with the wildlife technician who knew the county much better than I could hope to.

We sat down together the day before the season opener to plan out how we would work on opening day. We decided to take a canoe down the Bark River east of Fort Atkinson. We would launch southwest of the Prince's Point wildlife area which was a popular duck hunting area.

We would soon learn that our plan faced some challenges. The fall had been exceptionally dry that year. The Bark River in the area didn't seem to have any visible movement to its flow. It was so low the river looked like stagnant water. However my partner advised that he knew where there were some private marshes not far inland from the river channel that always had duck hunters in them on opening day. He felt we would still find enough hunters to check.

With a noon opener, the day was fairly warm. Unfortunately the warm sunny day was not the best for duck hunting. There wasn't a lot of shooting around us. We were several miles from the boat landing late in the day. We decided to listen for late shooting in the private marshes. Closing time came and went without much shooting. We chose to begin our long paddle back to the boat landing.

While we were underway we suddenly heard a barrage of shots due north of our position. The shots were in the general area but were not close to the river channel. It was the only violation we had seen or heard all day so we decided to work inland through a thick brushy swamp. We tied up the canoe on the bank and began to work our way towards the shots.

The walk was tough as the light began to fade during our struggle through the thick brush. It was now more than 15 minutes after closing time and multiple rounds of shots continued to ring out from the area in front of us. We finally reached an area where the brush began to become less dense. We saw some ducks flying over a pond in front of us. A man yelled, "Shoot now!" Three quick loud shotgun blasts shattered the evening sky followed by a man laughing hard in what almost sounded like a cackle. We kind of looked at each other wondering what was going on in front of us. We stood silently in the brush to gather more evidence of the violation.

"Here they come, shoot now," a man yelled! Another three shots boomed away. Once again we heard a man laughing like he was truly enjoying himself. We walked out in the open area around the pond to see an older gentleman sitting in a lawn chair looking up at the sky. A much younger man was hiding behind a bush farther down the edge of the pond. The younger man saw us approach and walked over to meet us. He was not carrying a shotgun. Meanwhile the older man continued to look skyward not realizing we were near.

We displayed our warden credentials and told the younger man we were checking hunting licenses. I also asked if the man knew it was after hunting hours. The younger man apologized and said he was trying to help his grandfather to kill a duck. We looked at the older man and realized he still didn't know we were there. He must have heard someone talking because he looked up at the sky and yelled, "Where?"

The younger man brought us to his grandfather and told him the game wardens were here. As I began to talk to the grandfather it was obvious he was almost deaf. I had to yell so he could hear me ask for his hunting license. As he pulled out his hunting license I noticed he was wearing blue bib overalls and white tennis shoes, not the normal duck hunting outfit.

I nearly fell over when I looked at his hunting license. It said he was born in 1894. I had never checked a date of birth on a hunting license that began with an 1800 number. I looked at his grandson and asked if his grandfather was in fact 88 years old? The grandson said that yes the old man was that old and was also nearly blind and deaf. He advised he had to yell when to shoot because his grandfather couldn't see the ducks very well. The younger man would simply yell "shoot now," when ducks came over the pond and the old man would shoot at whatever movement he could see in the evening sky. So far he had not hit anything but was having a great time based on how he laughed every time he shot at something.

I told the younger man it was time to quit for the day and to keep closer tabs on his grandfather's hunting hours in the future. He agreed to do so. We then began to make our way back towards the river.

The walk back through the thick swamp was much more challenging in the dark. We sort of meandered our way around the thicker spots until we hit the river. Unfortunately, when we got to the river, we did not return to where we had left the canoe. To make matters worse, we didn't know if the canoe was upstream or downstream. It took us more than an hour to finally find our ride home. The low water conditions also made the paddle back take much longer than normal.

It was 10pm when we reached the boat landing. My supervisor was still at the boat landing wondering why it was taking so long for his new warden to get back. We shared our experiences with him over a very late meal, while also planning our pre-dawn work detail for the next day's hunt.

It was hardly an auspicious beginning for me on my first waterfowl opener as the warden in Jefferson County. Yet as time went on, something made me think back to that day. It wasn't the thick swamp, the lost canoe, or the long paddle home. I instead remember the fun the old man was having; banging away with his 12 gauge shotgun at shadows in the sky. Someday I hope I am still having that much fun in the outdoors when I am 88 years old.

11 Deer Decoys; The Demise of Road Hunting

The most common complaint through the first half of my career during the deer gun season was of hunters shooting at deer from the highway. Farmers in particular had to endure rifle fire on to their pastures and woodlands. Some hunters would fire bullets over horses and dairy cows in pastures in an attempt to hit deer a longer distance from the road. There were even landowners who had road hunters shoot at them when a deer passed between their deer stand and the roadway.

Stopping road hunting during these early years was not easy. Many hunters drove down the road in their vehicle with only a partially cased weapon in one hand and a loaded magazine or clip in the other. When a deer was spotted in an adjacent field or clearing, the driver would stop and the passenger would have the rifle loaded in seconds. Likewise if a warden attempted to stop a vehicle suspected of road hunting, the man holding the rifle could remove the magazine and zip the gun case closed before the vehicle rolled to a stop.

Because of the short amount of time it took poachers to unload and case weapons, young warden recruits were often evaluated on how fast they could jump from their trainer warden's vehicle and get to the suspect vehicle. The trainer warden expected the recruit to rush up to the vehicle before the bad guys could unload their guns. Many other law enforcement officers would shake their heads at the practice wondering why any officer would want to get to a vehicle while the guns were still loaded! Wardens were definitely unique in that regard.

During the 1980's, some road hunters stretched the meaning of the word gun case as well. Some enterprising hunters began using ladies' nylons as gun cases. When questioned by a warden, the hunter would simply say the gun is enclosed so you can't write me a ticket. This eventually led to a revamp of the gun case definition in Wisconsin. The new rule stated that the firearm must be totally enclosed in a case designed to carry a firearm and must be enclosed with zipper, buckles, or ties. This ended the ladies' nylon defense.

Road hunting was a problem at night as well. Wardens working nighttime road hunters began to use reflective devices to entice the road hunters to shine a spotlight where the wardens were watching the area. They would assign a less senior warden to run across the road in front of the approaching poacher vehicle at a distance just at the outside range of the vehicle headlights. The young warden would carry a small board with a small reflector on it as he dashed across the road. The poacher would get a glimpse of the reflection and would believe the headlights were reflecting off the eyes of a deer. The vehicle would then stop in the approximate location and would cast the spotlight to try to illuminate and shoot the deer. This would give the wardens in the chase car the reason to stop the vehicle to check for weapons.

Other wardens began to refine this technique by using thin wires with reflectors on the ends of the wire. The wires would be connected to a small battery powered motor that would raise the wire and reflectors in a road ditch as the vehicle approached, thus imitating the eyes of a deer as well. Wardens began to use remote controlled devices to move the wires while still seated in their trucks.

However in the end, what poachers wanted the most was something to shoot at. Many arrests were made by wardens hiding their vehicle near a field with live deer present. However, some nights the deer would not cooperate so the wardens had to find another option. A few experimented with propping up dead car-killed deer which drew in a few shots. But it was the deer decoy developed in the late 1980's that really changed the game between poacher and warden.

I purchased a deer decoy for work in 1988. Because Jefferson County only had a 5 day deer season at that time, I was always assigned to work in another county the second weekend of the season. In this particular year, I was assigned to work in Iowa County in far southwestern Wisconsin. I arrived with my deer decoy in the back of the truck. Iowa County hunters had not experienced a deer decoy before.   Therefore our success was nearly guaranteed.

The local warden had a long list of landowners who had called in past complaints about people shooting deer illegally on their land from vehicles. He had no problem finding landowners who would give us permission to place the deer decoy on private land. We would always pick a field that had multiple "No Trespassing" signs posted along the road so that the judge would have no question about the kind of hunters we were dealing with.

We had the deer decoy in the first field for only a few minutes when a vehicle skidded to a halt in front of us. As the hunters were quickly exiting the vehicle to shoot, another car came along. Both groups of road hunters were now in a race to see who was going to shoot the deer first. The "No Trespassing" signs had no influence on either party. Multiple hunters were on the road with their guns pointed at the deer when the first shot was fired. Fortunately for us, we were using a video camera to record the effectiveness of the deer decoy. Having the camera allowed us to play back the tape to confirm which of the hunters actually fired the first shot.

We soon learned that in those early years of decoy use, multiple chase cars were required. We found that before a warden could finish writing a citation to one hunting group stopped down the road, another group would be in front of the decoy shooting again. After making a half dozen arrests in one location we would need to move to another farm because by that time word would be out at local bars that the wardens were using a fake deer in a particular field.

Some people simply could not believe that the decoy was a fake deer. Some hunters would stare at the deer even after receiving their citation and still believe it was a real deer. On one occasion we also had an ethical hunter give us a chance to laugh at the decoy's effectiveness. We were seated in our truck in the landowner's yard, waiting for the warden watching the decoy to radio us of a shot fired. A vehicle pulled into the driveway where we were sitting with our blaze orange jackets on. A hunter was in the car. He pulled up next to our truck and told us there was a nice buck down the road. He emphasized that we should hurry before the deer runs off. We nodded and told him we would be leaving soon. Five minutes later the man came back and with more urgency told us the buck was still there and had only moved about 20 feet from where it first was! He was almost pleading with us to come and shoot that deer. He seemed quite perplexed that we were so nonchalant about getting a buck. The warden sitting across the road from the decoy advised the man stopped and looked at the decoy a third time shaking his head that those dumb hunters up the road wouldn't come to shoot the buck.

Some of the hunters who were stopped for shooting the decoy were quite irate. We stopped one man who had just shot the decoy with a 30-06 rifle from inside the truck. After identifying ourselves as wardens we asked the man for his rifle. He yelled at us that we were not going to touch his rifle as he lunged for the weapon. I was at the open passenger door, so when he lunged for the rifle I did the same thing. Because I was standing I had more leverage and yanked the rifle towards me out of the man's hands, barrel forward. It was a split second reaction with no time to think. When a man lunges for a weapon, you want to do everything possible to make sure he does not complete the task. As I stepped back from the truck, I found the safety off with a live round in the chamber. If the rifle had discharged during the tussle over it, the 30-06 round would have gone through my bullet proof vest like a hot knife through butter. Our vests were only designed to stop handgun rounds.

On another day in Iowa County we met another unhappy customer. After a truck stopped in front of the decoy, the passenger stepped out and shot over the hood of the truck at the decoy. The decoy was again placed behind a "No Trespassing" sign. I was driving the chase car, so I quickly drove my truck to the area and stopped the vehicle with lights and siren as it left the scene. Before I could say anything the driver was yelling at me that he was going to have me arrested for reckless driving. I continued to do my work which included documenting the information off the rifle used to shoot from the road. I then issued the citation to the shooter. The man who had shot was the son-in-law of the driver. The driver was the local police chief from a nearby community. He got quite a bit of flak for his involvement in the road hunting episode.

During one day of decoy use in LaCrosse County, I had to protect the decoy from an unexpected attack. We had cited a man for hunting from the road about 20 minutes earlier. I was back in my hiding spot behind some thick cedar trees on a steep hill on the side of the road opposite from the decoy. I was hidden there waiting to radio the wardens in the chase car when someone would shoot at the decoy.

Two hunters in a truck pulled to a stop in front of me. The passenger jumped out of the truck with a spray can of orange paint. He was the same man who had been cited earlier. He crawled over the barbed wire fence, past the "No Trespassing" sign and started to run across the pasture towards the deer decoy approximately 125 yards away. He intended to spray our decoy orange so that it could not be used to nab any more road hunters.

I yelled for the man to stop as I skidded down the slope on to the road. He just kept going. I leaped over the fence and started sprinting after the man. I called the wardens in the chase car for assistance because I didn't like the fact that I also had a man behind me with a rifle. The man running towards the decoy was surprised when I grabbed him 10 yards short of the decoy. He didn't know I had been a sprinter on the track team in high school and college. The man was arrested for obstructing a warden which carried a much higher penalty than the earlier charge of hunting from a road.

We also discovered that some poachers will try anything to maintain their method of poaching. We had one such incident in northern LaCrosse County, following a very productive day with a deer decoy on one farmer's land. Later that night the landowner received death threats on the phone for allowing wardens to use decoys on his land to stop road hunting. Apparently the poachers felt they were entitled to poach deer on other people's land.

After about five years of decoy use, road hunters changed their ways. Some just gave up, resigned to the fact that the days of easy road hunting were gone. However the hard core poachers simply refined their techniques. They followed a procedure in which they would not shoot unless the deer moved first. In the early years, wardens only used stationary decoys. This new development required the wardens to also refine their technique. Thus the motorized decoy was created.

Motorized decoys used two small remote controlled motors placed at the tail and the neck of the decoy. With a remote control box, the warden watching the decoy could twitch the tail or could slowly rotate the head of the deer decoy. This little bit of movement was usually enough for the poachers to open fire. Eventually movement alone could not get poachers to shoot. We began to see poachers stop to blow their car horn at deer or to whistle at deer standing motionless in a field. When the deer did not move the poachers would laugh at the wardens and would drive away. Of course we would have the last laugh as the real deer would then take a few steps and continue eating.

The year after I retired I found it unfortunate and ironic that the state legislature passed a law allowing hunters to drive down the road with uncased rifles in their vehicles. It appears some people need to learn the lessons of the past all over again. Arrests for shooting from the highway jumped the following deer season but publicity about that fact was not allowed to be stressed in the DNR deer season report for political reasons.

12 Mostly Friendly Catfish Anglers

I sometimes wonder why people fishing for catfish were always the friendliest fishermen. It seemed like no one wanted to shake my hand more when I checked fishing licenses than the people fishing for catfish. Not wanting to be rude, I would shake hands with any angler who wanted to shake my hand. However shaking hands with someone fishing for catfish had a very obvious physical consideration.

Catfish bait is called stink bait for good reason. Many anglers had their own concoctions of catfish bait. The worse it smelled the more confidence they had that it would attract catfish. Shaking hands with someone with catfish bait all over their hands was an experience that stayed with me the rest of the day; no matter how many times I washed my hands.

There was one exception to the friendly reaction I received from the catfishing crowd. One day I scanned Lake Koshkonong with my binoculars and noticed an unusual sight. I spotted an anchored boat with one occupant. Even though there was only one person on-board, the boat looked like a porcupine. Fishing rods were propped up in every part of the boat. The legal limit of fishing lines per person is three in Wisconsin. However this boat had out at least three times as many. The bright sun reflected off the monofilament line from the poles showing lines extending into the water 360 degrees around the boat.

This posed a challenge from a navigation perspective. I needed to approach the boat without running over lines. The number of lines made this impossible. I figured I would have to drive up to the boat slower than my normal approach to avoid entangling my lower unit of the boat motor in fishing line. I approached from behind the occupant who was facing away from me and was wearing a straw hat. I also noticed cigar smoke rising into the air from the angler.

As I boated to within fifty yards of the boat, the occupant turned around to look at me approaching. I was surprised to see that the occupant was a large woman. When her eyes met mine, she pulled the cigar from her mouth and began burning through the monofilament line on her extra lines as quickly as possible. She knew she had too many lines out and was taking action to burn the lines with her cigar so the lines would not be counted against her. The tightness of the lines in the poles quickly pulled the burned off portion out of the poles before they quickly sank to the bottom.

I accelerated to try to salvage the evidence of the violation. The occupant kept burning lines off as I pulled alongside. I identified myself as a conservation warden and told the woman to leave the lines alone. She burned off a few more and then sat back in her boat seat, feeling comfortable that she had destroyed the evidence. I asked the woman for her fishing license and told her she was in violation for fishing with too many lines. She responded that she was only fishing with three lines and put the cigar back in to her mouth and crossed her arms in front of her in defiance.

Mollie was not the most cooperative angler I would ever meet. She would confess to nothing. I was unable to check the lines she had burned through to determine if they were baited or even had hooks on and she knew it. I told her to reel in the remaining three poles to check to see if only one hook was on each line. That was in fact what each pole had. Just when I thought all was lost my eye caught a glimpse of some monofilament tied around an oar lock. I pulled up the line and retrieved a baited hood. I told Mollie, "You forgot this one," and took out my citation book.

Molly blew cigar smoke in the air but didn't say much more.

After I issued the citation, I pulled away and continued my patrol. I figured I would never see Mollie again. Mollie didn't pay her citation nor did she appear in court. A warrant for her arrest was issued by the court. A year later, I was checking shore fishermen in Jefferson along the Rock River. I was surprised to see Mollie sitting on a bucket, fishing from shore. I asked to see her fishing license. With license in hand I asked Mollie if she remembered me. She was quite to the point. She referred to me as that warden with the bad attitude!

I decided to run a check with the dispatcher to see if the warrant for Mollie was still active. The dispatcher confirmed the warrant was still an active one. I informed Mollie that she was under arrest for failing to pay her past citation. I transported her to the county jail. I was met by a new jail matron who was putting in her first day on the job. For months after that she reminded me how she was not real happy with me for dropping off a cigar smoking, tough talking woman on her first day of work. She also emphasized the point of being required to search the new jail resident's body for contraband that posed quite a challenge due to the prisoner's heavy build. Mollie apparently chose another county to fish in after getting out of jail, because I never saw Mollie again after that.

13 Shooting Geese can be Costly

Most waterfowl hunters hunt the state's marshes, lakes, and rivers in pursuit of their ducks. After all, waterfowl are supposed to be on the water. However a few lucky hunters also find feeding areas inland; where ducks and geese stuff themselves on scattered grain left behind by the corn combine.

One day I was driving through the cropland of Jefferson County north of Lake Koshkonong near Busseyville. A few hunters had patterned ducks and geese as the birds left the lake on their daily flights inland to feed. However I was only watching for flights of ducks on this day. It was a year in which the goose season was quite short. This was a week that was open for duck hunting but not goose hunting.

I saw a truck parked near a picked corn field so I figured a duck hunter was somewhere nearby. I parked my truck on a dead end road and walked through some standing corn to see if I could locate the hunter. As I looked over the picked cornfield with my binoculars, I saw a hunter lying on his back. He sat up from time to time to scan the sky in all directions around him.

The call of geese in the distance caused the man to drop flat against the ground. Through my binoculars I could see him wiggling to make himself invisible. I still didn't expect much as the geese approached because the goose season was closed. As the small flock of geese swung over the man's location, he suddenly sat up and swung on the birds with his shotgun. I was surprised when the man fired at the geese. I was more surprised when he only fired one time. I thought to myself that if he was going to shoot geese out of season, he would at least fire three shots instead of one.

After a few seconds the geese flew out of sight and the man stood up and began walking back to his truck. Had the man's conscience got to him for his illegal act? I walked back to my truck and drove towards the man's truck so I could intercept him before he left the area. As he reached the pavement, I climbed out of my truck and identified myself as a conservation warden. I immediately saw the reason why the man had only fired one shot. The man's shotgun barrel was destroyed. The muzzle end of the shotgun barrel had peeled back nearly 8 inches, separating into 6 strips of metal that had peeled back perpendicular to the rest of the barrel.

As I looked at the man's hunting license, I asked him why he was shooting at geese since the hunting season was closed. The man sort of shrugged his shoulders. He didn't have a good answer. The man knew the season was closed. I then asked him, "What happened to your shotgun?"

The man stated that as he was trying to get as close to the ground as possible to hide from the approaching geese, he apparently had pushed the end of the shotgun barrel into the soft ground. With the barrel plugged with mud, the barrel could not handle the build-up in pressure from the shotgun blast when it pushed against the obstruction. I asked the man if I could take a photo of the shotgun to use as a teaching tool in local hunter safety classes. The man reluctantly agreed.

I then informed the man that since he had shot at geese during the closed season he would be receiving a citation for that offense. The man pleaded with me to not issue a citation because he was one of the officers in a local Ducks Unlimited Chapter. I responded that as an officer in that organization he should lead by example and should not be shooting birds out of season. The man quietly accepted the citation and walked to his truck with his destroyed shotgun. In the end, the man was actually lucky. He could have been blinded or killed if the barrel had ruptured closer to his head. However I doubt that he felt very lucky as he drove home that day adding up the costs of the citation and a new shotgun barrel.

14 Sweating it out to Catch Fish Poachers

Randy, the warden from Watertown, called me at my home in Jefferson to ask if I could help him to work a complaint. It was August which tends to be a quieter month for warden work. Usually the fishing isn't the best during the dog days of summer. By August, most wardens are also getting tired of working boating enforcement. I asked what kind of complaint this was going to be.

Randy advised that he had information that a small group of men were running illegal set lines or drop lines on the Rock River. An informant had told the warden that the men were from Illinois and that one of men had a criminal record for sexual assault. Randy told me he had run a check on the man and had confirmed that fact. According to the information given, the men were tying dozens of baited lines to the ends of tree limbs overhanging the river in an attempt to catch catfish. This would be a violation for both fishing with too many lines as well as leaving lines unattended. Commercial setline licenses were not available for fishing in Jefferson County. The men were using a small motorboat to move up and down the river after dark to conduct their illegal activity. Because the river isn't wide enough to hide a boat in the area, one of us would need to be watching the river on foot.

As we looked over the situation, we decided where we would need to watch the area from. This was an area with crop fields and grassy areas lining the river. It would not be difficult to find a place to hide. However there was another concern. Since this was a very hot part of the summer, the wet vegetated areas along the river would be prime mosquito breeding areas.

We also decided that if the warden on foot observed the illegal activity, the warden in the chase boat would stop to pick up the warden on foot. We felt this was a wise strategy to follow before pursuing the suspects, due to the criminal record of at least one of the men. Stopping the suspect boat in a remote area such as this one would mean that back-up from the Sheriff's department would take a very long time to get there.

I agreed to take the first night on foot. I thought about my options to protect my body from the swarms of mosquitoes that I knew would be waiting. Despite the heat, I decided to wear light weight rain gear the mosquitoes could not bite through. I also wore a warden hat with a mesh head net over the top. For the final step, I wore a thin pair of canvas gloves with liberal amounts of mosquito repellent sprayed over my hands and head.

I found a flat spot to sit on a folding seat I brought along with me. I sat down in a corn field, two rows in from the edge of the stream. The corn was head high at this time which offered plenty of concealment. Being in position just before dark, I prepared myself for what would be a long wait. As darkness settled in, squadrons of mosquitoes rallied themselves in search of fresh blood. My selection of clothing was working well as far as preventing hundreds of mosquito bites. However listening to the steady buzzing of dozens of mosquitoes around my head for several hours nearly drove me crazy. The heat was also an obvious problem. The lack of air circulation through my rain gear made me conscious of the drops of sweat running down my back beneath my bullet-proof vest. Although it was now after dark, the temperature was still in the 80's.

It was at times like this that I would think about people who made comments to me in the past about what an easy job I had. "All you have to do is ride around in a boat all day!" I wondered how many of those people would be willing to join me now in the mosquito infested heat, waiting for a violent criminal to appear in the darkness.

At around 11pm, I caught a glimpse of flashlights on the stream to my right. I radioed to the other warden that I had some activity working towards me. Several minutes later a boat came quietly down the river without the required navigation lights. As one man operated the small outboard motor, the other two men were tying baited lines to tree branches hanging down over the river. The lines were each several feet long, allowing the bait to hang down into the water column near the bottom of the shallow stream. The men were very busy tying lines as they continued out of sight to my left.

I radioed to Randy that it was time to take the men down. As the suspect boat went out of sight downstream, I began to hear the outboard motor approaching from upstream at a high rate of speed. As Randy got close, I flipped my flashlight briefly on in his direction so he would know where to pick me up. The warden boat was on plane, coming at me at full throttle. As Randy throttled down to approach my location on shore, the boat unfortunately ran aground in the muddy flats. Water and mud flew in all directions as the motor's propeller threw mud and water into the air. With great effort, we pushed and pulled on the boat until it slid back into the deeper river channel. Randy then lowered the outboard motor into the water and brought the boat back on plane. In less than two minutes we saw the flashlights working ahead of us.

As we maneuvered our boat next to the suspect boat, we were definitely on alert. This is the critical time for a law enforcement officer. Were the suspects armed? What was their state of mind? Would they accept their fate peacefully or would they lose their temper and choose to fight or shoot?

When we asked the men about the lines tied to the tree branches, they stated that they didn't know anything about that. The men chose a strategy of acting as if they had done nothing wrong. They didn't know I had observed them from my hidden observation point. The men stated they were going to fish for catfish but had not done any fishing yet. I then informed the men they had tied lines to trees right in front of me while I was sitting in the cornfield. The men had nothing more to say. The men were then issued citations for the violations and bond was collected because the men were not residents of the state.

When Randy gave me a ride back to my truck after midnight, we were both hot and covered with mud. My uniform was soaked in sweat. I felt satisfied that we had apprehended the men in difficult working conditions. Yet I knew that other than the complainant, there probably wasn't anyone else in the county who would have an appreciation for the challenges their two game wardens had faced that night.

15 Defending the Capitol from Our Citizens

During the early months of 2011, I began to prepare for my retirement. I knew what my retirement date was going to be. I had submitted my retirement paperwork and had picked a date in April. I was trying to tie up loose ends so that my replacement would not have to deal with a lot of extra work when he or she arrived in my office at some later date.

In contrast to my plans, there existed a different backdrop at the State Capitol in Madison. Governor Walker had been sworn into office in January. The Republican Party now had control of the Assembly, Senate, and the Governor's mansion. As a result of this concentration of political power, things began to change. Rumors were flying around through state offices across Wisconsin about what the party in control was going to do to state employees. Most of the state employee unions had supported the Democratic candidate for Governor. Some were concerned that since they had bet on the losing horse in the race, it would now be hell to pay. In some ways they were not far off.

In February, discussions began to take place over the Governor's plan to "decertify" the state employee and state teacher unions. In other words, the Governor was going to eliminate collective bargaining that had existed for many decades prior to my career.

Like many people I had mixed emotions about unions. I was in a union as a field warden. I was not in a union the last two thirds of my career as a supervisor because I was considered to be a member of the management team. As a supervisor, I worked with many very dedicated people over my career. However, I also had some bad experiences with a very small number of union employees doing unethical things. When I tried to address the issues to hold those people accountable, I was over-ruled at a higher level in state government which left me very frustrated.

I knew the individuals were violating the public's trust and the union was doing everything possible to make sure the employees were not held accountable. Part of their strategy was to make false accusations against both my supervisor and me. Despite those experiences, I still felt that ethical and honest public employees and teachers should have the right to collectively bargain for some basic benefits such as wages and work place safety. However my feelings were not going to matter as the calendar turned to March of 2011.

When word spread about the legislative plan to end collective bargaining in Wisconsin, it was obvious that a lot of workers would descend on Madison to exercise their freedom of speech on the issue. A planning team of managers in the Capitol Police, University Police, DNR, and State Patrol soon recognized that security at the State Capitol would be an issue. Since field level officers in these agencies were also union members, there was a concern as to whether or not it would be wise to assign officers to protect legislators who would be taking away the same officers' rights. The alternate plan at least for DNR employees; would be to use only management personnel to protect the Capitol because management staff did not belong to a union. There were far fewer management level officers than field officers, so people in my position had to put in several weeks of security duty at the Capitol.

The State Patrol continued to use their troopers for security details because the Governor had exempted the State Patrol from the Collective Bargaining bill. It was more than a coincidence that the State Patrol served as the Governor's security team. Governor Walker must have known what was coming because he tripled the size of the Governor's security team with troopers when he took office.

My first week at the Capitol was uneventful. Many thousands of teachers, firemen, highway workers, and university staff came to the Capitol to carry signs to protest and to meet with their local legislators. Democratic legislators had their doors open but most Republican legislators kept their doors locked. About the only thing the protestors asked of us was "Where are the restrooms?" Everyone was very well behaved and courteous. It was a stark contrast to the protestors I dealt with in northern Wisconsin during the spear fishing protests of the late 1980's. Then again, you wouldn't expect problems from kindergarten teachers.

As I was finishing my second week at the Capitol, the atmosphere changed dramatically. Crowds began to swell outside the Capitol. At times as many as 125,000 people were estimated to be circling the Capitol square. Then to make matters worse, busloads of Republican supporters from other states including Tea Party groups began to appear. After each 12 hour shift, I would return to a local hotel room to watch the live broadcast of a national cable news show called "The Ed Show," taking place outside my hotel on the Capitol square.

Tensions began to steadily build as the entire country began to see this as having a potential impact on the middle class throughout the United States. Some young people from the University of Wisconsin refused to leave the Capitol, sleeping on the marble floors in sleeping bags. At one point, the Governor's office pushed for a shutdown of the Capitol. The Capitol Police then instructed all protestors that beginning the next day, a 5pm closure of the Capitol would take effect. What we didn't know was that this was setting the stage for a very quick and unexpected vote in the following days.

When the Republicans called for a vote to end collective bargaining, it was done without warning late in the day. I had been tasked during my 12 hour shift to provide direction to a group of police officers from small communities around Wisconsin. The night the vote was suddenly called, was the same day these extra officers were sent home early because no one in the command post had expected anything to happen the remainder of the evening. Therefore, when word spread across Madison that a vote was taking place on the collective bargaining bill, we were not fully staffed. As we looked out of the Capitol windows and entrance doors we could see large numbers of people massing on the streets as they began to make their way up the streets to our location. It was like watching colonies of ants descending on us from the distance. The doors of the Capitol were locked since it was now after 5pm.

With the doors locked, the determined masses tried everything to gain entry into the Capitol. The doors were rumbling from people pounding on them from the outside. One very anxious legislative staff member came up to me and said, "There are men trying to crawl through the window of the ladies room!"

Being on the ground floor, I immediately went into the ladies' restroom and found the window open about a foot with several men trying to open it enough to crawl through. I was able to push them back but found the lock on the window was no longer holding. I had nothing to use to keep it closed except my own body. Not having any other option, I stepped up on to the window sill and placed my other foot on the middle of the window frame to hold it down.

People outside the window kept yelling at me to let them in but they did not attempt to break the window. As I stood on the window frame, I wondered if I had finally reached the pinnacle of my career; defending the ladies' restroom from invasion! Within minutes the command post radioed to all officers in the Capitol that we should withdraw from our positions to one of the upper floors to regroup.

When I left the restroom I could understand why the order was made. Protestors had found other holes in the defenses and were pouring into the building. We went to an upper floor until another group of officers from outside of Madison could be called up to relieve us several hours later. By the time I left the Capitol that night I had been on duty for more than 14 hours. One estimate suggested that 25000 protestors had entered the building during the final charge. Every level of the building was packed with people. Fortunately, it was a very peaceful protest. There was no violence to deal with.

The following morning I received a telephone call from the DNR command post. They asked me if I wanted to do a third week of duty at the Capitol. I declined as did some other supervisors. Field wardens were then offered shifts on a volunteer basis.

Retiring at a time of such turmoil in my home state was a disappointment after a more than thirty year career in public service. I had been a resident of the state my entire life. I did not approve of the manner in which some legislators were leading in order to push through their agenda. Public service was a concept that appeared to be foreign to some of the legislators I escorted through the hallways. During my time in the Capitol I heard legislators make disparaging comments about public workers at the same time they were expecting me to protect them from harm.

One leader of the Assembly had hand-picked the largest

troopers at the Capitol to protect him while in the chambers. He didn't need protection from the public, he was asking for protection from his fellow legislators. It was a sad commentary on how toxic the environment among our elected officials had become. I saw no desire for compromise from the party in power. The strategy was to do whatever it took to win instead of doing everything possible to do what was right.

A month later I turned in my gear and removed the badge from my chest for the last time. My time in the Capitol was over. However the legacy of this legislature is still being played out in weakened environmental laws, the shifting in taxpayer funds from public schools to private schools, and in enabling private corporations to write their own legislation. I wonder how historians fifty years into the future will describe the conservation of our natural resources during this decade of Wisconsin's leadership.

16 The Grandfathers of Walleye Poaching

It was an early spring day in March of 1997. The call of migrating Sandhill cranes and Canada geese could be heard in the skies above. The Mississippi River's main navigation channel had shed its ice and was now a channel of open water. Walleye anglers were out in significant numbers fishing from boats. It had been a milder winter that had enabled open water fishing for an extended period of time below some of the local locks and dams on the river. Throughout these months with open water, wardens at the LaCrosse DNR office had received numerous citizen complaints about two brothers taking more than their legal limit of saugers and walleyes.

The Mississippi River is unique as far as bag limits are concerned for Wisconsin fishermen. On this Wisconsin/Minnesota boundary portion of the river, anglers can take a combination of 6 walleye and/or sauger per day which is more than inland anglers may take. You would think that taking 6 walleyes a day would be enough. However these two brothers wanted to take more. In fact in some weeks, people were so upset with the two brothers that the DNR office was getting complaints from five or six different people per week about the two men's activities.

The two brothers were retired, both in their 70's, and had a lot of time on their hands. They also had a lot of river fishing experience. They had seen many wardens come and go in their lifetime and had studied warden routines to avoid getting caught. Catching the two brothers would be a challenge.

Wardens in the LaCrosse area held a meeting to address the issue and to develop an investigative plan. The wardens decided to follow a schedule where different wardens would take either a morning or afternoon shift at the Genoa, Dresbach, and Trempealeau dams on the Mississippi River. The suspects were known to fish at all three dams. We had no idea which dam the brothers would go to for their second fishing trip of the day.

Once at their assigned dam, each warden was to look for the two brothers and their known fishing companions. Any warden finding the suspects was to document where the suspects were fishing, what boats they were using, whose vehicle had been used, companions the suspects were fishing with, their clothing descriptions, and what fish had been observed to be caught. The wardens would then do a mid-day briefing to the other wardens starting the later shift to share the information. This investigation method was in response to the citizen complaints that the two brothers were making multiple fishing trips per day in order to take multiple bag limits per day.

On the first morning of the coordinated investigation, I was hidden at a location near the Dresbach dam. The younger of the two brothers launched a boat with a known fishing companion at around 8am that morning. They were using the companion's boat and truck. I conducted surveillance of the men for four hours. I was able to document that they had kept at least 11 walleyes or saugers. When the men loaded their boat and left the landing, I followed the vehicle from a safe distance until they reached the companion's home. I then waited to see what vehicle was driven away from the home by the youngest brother. I documented that he left with his own vehicle. I then passed on the information from the morning investigation to the other wardens on the team.

The warden assigned to the Dresbach dam in the afternoon soon spotted the same brother returning to the dam to fish. This time the same brother arrived with his own truck and boat. After catching 4 more walleyes, the man came in to the boat landing several hours later at which time the warden contacted him. After the warden counted out the 4 walleyes, he told the man he wanted to talk to him about the fish he had caught in the morning. The man didn't lie but he didn't tell the truth either. He simply responded that he wasn't out with this boat in the morning. The warden then advised the suspect that he knew he wasn't out with his own boat in the morning, he had been out with his companion in his companion's boat and that he needed to see those fish.

The suspect admitted he had fish at home. I was already parked up the street from the man's residence with another warden, waiting for a radio call from the warden at the Dresbach dam. When the radio confirmation came that fish from the morning were at the home, we contacted the man's wife and asked to see the man's morning catch. The wife took us out to the garage and showed us a pail with 6 walleyes inside. The fish had not been cleaned yet. We then asked to see the fish in the freezer in the house. We collected those fish as well. We had all of the man's fish by the time he returned home.

Meanwhile, the other wardens on the team were visiting the home of the older brother. The other brother was home and also had 6 walleyes in a pail that were not cleaned yet. Upon examining freezers in his home, a large number of walleyes were found in many packages of fish. Between the two brothers, wardens were able to document 210 walleyes and saugers in their possession, which was well over the combined possession limit for the two men of 24 fish. The men were charged for the violations, paid more than a $1000 in fines, and lost their fishing privileges for several years despite their advanced age.

In warden lingo, these men would be called "fish hogs." These are people who take much more than they legally can keep when fish are most vulnerable. To other anglers, this situation came down to a basic case of fairness. If the men had simply caught a limit each day, and gone home, no one would have complained. However by taking multiple bag limits of fish per day, they were insulting the values of the anglers fishing in other boats around them. In the end, it was a perfect example of concerned citizens helping wardens to do their job by reporting serious violations.

We also had this kind of support at the Trempealeau dam on the Mississippi River. A concerned caller informed us in October of 2000 that walleyes and saugers were being caught in large numbers below the dam. The caller advised he had also seen some boats of anglers make multiple trips the day before. Because the Trempealeau warden was out of town on that day, I recruited a part-time warden to accompany me to the dam early the next morning. The caller had been correct. The fish were really biting.

We took a position on shore where we could observe the people in boats with our binoculars. We soon noticed one boat with three occupants was doing exceedingly well. The men kept 18 saugers before returning to the boat landing. They had only been gone for about an hour when they returned for their second trip. The men then caught an additional 16 sauger before we launched a boat late in the afternoon to contact the men on the water.

After asking for their fishing licenses we counted the men's fish and placed them in our boat. We then informed the men we had watched them catch their morning limit and needed to have those fish as well. Without giving the men time to argue the fact, I told them to follow us to the landing. The men complied without saying a word. Because all three men were from southeastern

Wisconsin, they were staying in the local hotel. That would be our next destination. All of the morning fish were seized from the hotel and the men were cited and released. They also lost their fishing privileges for one year. Out of town anglers should be the last people to try poaching wild fish or game. They don't know who the people are in the boats around them.

On the other hand, some local anglers don't normally engage in this type of illegal activity unless they know they have an edge. One local angler thought he was safe to try double-tripping at the Genoa dam the night of the spring conservation hearings. These hearings take place every April to provide an opportunity for the public to provide input to potential changes in hunting and fishing regulations proposed by the DNR or the Conservation Congress. Local anglers know that wardens run these meetings so there is at least the perception that illegal actions may go undetected for a few hours while the hearings are taking place. Knowing this, I sometimes would work in the field during the spring hearings if I knew game fish were still being caught in large numbers during the spring fish run.

During April of 1997, on the morning of the spring hearings, I observed a man fishing off the wall at the Genoa dam. When the man left he had his limit of walleyes and sauger. I suspected he might return in the evening, so I also returned to fish from shore that night with camouflage rain gear over my uniform. As the man left with his second limit of fish that evening, he was quite surprised to encounter a warden while the spring hearings were still in progress. This man also lost his fishing privileges for one year. Arrests of this type send a wave of awareness through local bars and eating establishments where fishermen hang out. Sometimes catching just one creative poacher can prevent a dozen other people from attempting a similar strategy.

17 Exotic Threats to Wisconsin's Outdoors

Some Wisconsin residents apparently do not learn from the lessons of history. Exotic introductions for the most part have not had a positive influence on Wisconsin's outdoors. For example, the common carp and English sparrow were first introduced to our state in the late 1800's. Starlings and the stinging German Yellow Jackets came in the 1900's. Yet some people still believe that they are qualified to introduce new species into the state. A prime example of this dangerous trend is the introduction of feral pigs of the Russian Boar variety.

Feral pigs have been present in Crawford County since 2002. They first appeared just down the road from a captive elk farm. The owner of that farm was subsequently charged with the introduction of the feral hogs some time later. A friend of the man provided a statement to investigators that he had assisted the farm owner in obtaining the feral hogs in Texas. However the friend of the man recanted his testimony during the trial. A caretaker of the property also testified that he observed the farm owner to arrive at the farm with an empty cattle trailer with fresh hog droppings inside at the same time the illegal release took place. However, the judge in Crawford County found the man not guilty. The same man was subsequently convicted of illegally importing game to the State of Illinois.

Other people have apparently also been interested in establishing a feral hog population in Wisconsin. Small groups of the feral hogs have been shot and killed in multiple counties stretching into northern Wisconsin. Fortunately, only the Crawford County population has hung on. Both the DNR and Department of Agriculture have worked diligently through trapping and night shooting to try to eliminate that small population. If the feral hog population expands across

Wisconsin it will have serious consequences to both the agricultural community and the hunting community.

If you believe feral hogs are a good thing, you simply need to talk to land owners in states from Missouri to Texas to grasp how significant a problem these animals have become. Literally millions of dollars a year are spent on feral hog control in some states. The hogs root up freshly planted corn fields, create hog wallows along streams causing severe erosion, and gobble down food sources utilized by deer and turkeys. They also add a safety concern to outdoor enthusiasts who unfortunately find themselves between a large sow and her litter. A large boar crippled by another hunter can also be a very dangerous beast to encounter.

If exotic animals are not enough to worry about, there is also the threat to our woodlands from exotic plants. I find it ironic that so much attention is paid to food plots by deer hunters while at the same time so little attention is directed at invasive plant species. There are woodlots within our state right now that are already dominated by invasive brush species like honeysuckle, buckthorn, multi-flora rose, and Japanese barberry. These invasive brush species are so dense that there will never be any oak regeneration in these areas unless the landowner does something to kill the invasive brush first.

Many of these species were sold for decades at private nurseries as ornamental plants. Because many of these species have berries as fruit, birds ingest the berries and then fly away to disperse the seeds in other areas in their droppings. The DNR is attempting to reclassify these various invasive plant species under new rules to prohibit the future sale of them to the public. However, if you own woodlands in Wisconsin, you need to monitor your forests to begin control efforts. Planting a food plot for deer will not mean much if you allow invasive brush to overtake your forest.

Invasive fish species are also a growing problem. A snakehead fish was discovered in the Rock River in southern Wisconsin. Asian carp are slowly spreading up the Mississippi River. Round gobies and other invasive fish that upset the food chain are in the Great Lakes. It is sad that it has come to this. Invasive species in ballast water of ocean going vessels have been known to be the source of these Great Lakes invasive species for decades. Yet the U.S. Department of Transportation and U.S. Coast Guard relied on the shipping industry to follow "voluntary" control measures for most of that time period. These "voluntary" measures have added dozens of invasive species to Lake Michigan since that time.

Likewise, U.S. Senators punished U.S. Fish and Wildlife staff who attempted to classify Asian carp as an injurious species which would have prohibited their importation or sale. I personally know the man in the U.S. Fish and Wildlife Service who attempted to protect the Mississippi River from the Asian carp threat. As a political favor to the aquaculture industry, a U.S. Senator from Missouri had the employee reassigned to another position where he could not be involved with invasive fish policy. The aquaculture interests wanted to use the foreign carp in their catfish ponds. When severe flooding spread over the Mississippi River valley in the early 1990's, the catfish ponds were overtopped by flood waters allowing the Asian carp to enter the main river. This is another painful example of how politics prevented natural resource personnel from doing the right thing.

18 Baiting Battles

There is a slogan among game wardens. Not all baiters are poachers but all poachers bait. Baiting is a very effective method of poaching if the rules are not followed. It is hard to believe it has come to this considering where Wisconsin was on the subject when I began my career as a warden.

In the early 1980's, there was no baiting of deer allowed. Salt blocks were prohibited. Typically hunting over salt was the only material we would find poachers hunting over at that time. However the train went off the tracks some years later. Now the genie is out of the bottle and nobody knows how to put it back. Examples of egregious baiting are now found throughout Wisconsin. Meanwhile some states like Minnesota still ban all baiting.

As I first indicated, not all baiters are poachers. There are situations where a small bait pile can be helpful to a quality hunt. For example with a young archer who cannot pull back a bow with a high draw weight, the young archer needs to shoot only at close range. Likewise there are aging members of hunting parties who may have cancer or other serious diseases that hamper how steady they can hold a rifle anymore. In these situations, drawing a deer closer for a killing shot is the goal.

However poaching over bait is an entirely different story. Wardens in some counties can point to a large number of trophy bucks being taken in the late archery season during nights with a bright moon. Based on the cases that are made with a very limited warden force, poachers are hunting over large bait piles on snow-covered ground at night. With lighted bow sites and the bright moon overhead, some archers are hunting through the night until a large buck comes in to the attractive illegal bait pile.

This technique is so effective at poaching large bucks, that most wardens recognize that this style of poaching is more common now than traditional poaching with a gun and a spotlight. A bright spotlight working across a field is easier to detect than the inaudible release of a bow string deep in the woods.

Hunting over bait piles after hours takes place across Wisconsin. It is even common near very populated areas. In the LaCrosse area a significant percentage of arrests for this type of violation take place in the area immediately surrounding the city. You could call this "suburban poaching." Some of the poachers are targeting trophy bucks that live in the fringe of cities where firearm hunting is restricted. The poachers place large bait piles in the wooded fringe of backyards where they can see their bow sites clearly in the background light from the city or suburban street lights.

In northern Wisconsin where snow depths can still be measured in feet instead of inches, late season baiting is very effective. If the hunter is not ethical, the unfair advantage of hunting over a large bait pile after dark will likely be fatal to tired trophy bucks coming in to feed after another deer gun season.

Some poachers want all the comforts of home when they poach a deer at night over bait. We call those people "cabin shooters." These are people who place a bait pile or deer feeder behind their home or cabin within range of their preferred weapon. Some of these poachers will use a crossbow, while others prefer a relatively quiet round like a 22 caliber rifle. The cabin will usually will have one or more spotlights on the back of the building aimed at the bait. Some people will use motion activated sensors on the lights. When the light comes on in the backyard, the poacher will check to see if the deer is a "shooter" or a buck with a large enough rack to shoot. If it is, a window without a screen is slid open and the unsuspecting buck meets its end.

Cabin shooters are active across much of the state. Some cabin shooters also use the technique on bear and turkeys. It takes a lot of effort and man hours to apprehend these people. Some wardens will spend 20-30 nights in the fall working just one cabin shooter. It is a workload that can be very demanding when one considers that other warden work still has to be done during the day before another long night shift begins.

Another warden and I found a cabin shooting set-up in Monroe County in cranberry bog country. We found a cabin with a deer feeder, spotlights, and a window overlooking the backyard with no screens. However at the times we were there, no deer were taken. That isn't to say we were not successful. The owner of the cabin had such a desire to poach deer that he was also active in other ways.

The man was from the Chicago area and spoke with a strong eastern European accent. He could understand English, but during a series of arrests by wardens he always tried first to make believe he didn't understand a word. Roy, the Tomah warden at the time, was working with me a few miles from the cabin when we apprehended the man and two companions shining deer from their vehicle while in possession of a 22 caliber rifle.

The next opening day of deer season, Roy found the man hunting deer without a license and hunting without any blaze orange clothing. When we did a records check on the man, we also found he had a prior conviction for license fraud for buying a resident archery license as a nonresident. He also had a prior conviction and revocation of privileges for shining and shooting a deer a decade earlier. He is the kind of man a warden should follow when observed leaving a feed store with sacks of shell corn.

19 Talking Turkey

It was 1969 when my grandfather and I walked along an oak ridge in Marinette County during the deer gun season. I was a month short of turning 12 years old so I could not carry a gun or purchase a deer hunting license yet. I was accompanying my dad and grandfather to watch and to learn. As we walked along a deer trail below the top of the ridge, we flushed a large bird from an oak tree in front of us. After we watched it fly away we looked at each other with a surprised look in our faces. We had never seen such a bird in the woods before. We then realized we had flushed a wild turkey.

What we had seen in the woods that day was likely a turkey that had moved into the county from Upper Michigan. There had been attempts to establish turkeys in the area about that time. However the birds did not survive long in northeastern Wisconsin. Winters were a lot harder then and the birds did not have the right genetic strain to survive.

Young hunters today might find it hard to believe that when I was hired as a warden in 1980, there was no turkey hunting in Wisconsin. I was fortunate to work at time when efforts to re-establish the turkey population in Wisconsin were taking place. I was present at the first turkey release in eastern Jefferson County when individual birds were released from large cardboard boxes in the southern unit of the Kettle Moraine State Forest.

The turkeys that we hunt today originally came from the State of Missouri in a trade for ruffed grouse from Wisconsin. The first turkeys released in this program were stocked in Vernon County, south of LaCrosse. It is hard to find a better success story in wildlife management. Turkeys can now be hunted throughout

Wisconsin. In fact as I type this chapter on a cold March morning, I am watching a gobbler walk across the yard in front of my home. These opportunities did not exist 30 years ago.

In the early years after turkeys were first released, local residents were quite protective of them. People wanted the turkeys to survive. They didn't want anyone shooting them until the population became self-sustaining. In the early turkey hunting seasons, it seemed like the hunters who took the time to hunt them were also more ethical. However as turkey populations rose and more hunters began to pursue them, the sport attracted hunters who were not nearly as ethical.

Wardens began to notice this change before anyone else did. In fact we were perplexed that researchers in Wisconsin considered the illegal hen kill to be zero in the early years of their population models. We knew that wasn't accurate. Wardens were already receiving complaints of turkeys being shot from vehicles and hens being killed during the spring season. As deer baiting became more popular in the 1990's, wardens also were discovering illegal turkey baiting.

Some turkey poachers bait areas in front of their blind with corn. Others try to use something that is harder to spot from the air such as sunflower seeds. Some hunters simply spread large quantities of bird seed.

It was the information in turkey hunting accident reports that finally made researchers admit that there was an illegal hen harvest. Hunting accidents during the turkey season were becoming more common. The primary cause of the accidents was of hunters shooting at movement at what the hunter believed to be a turkey. Hunters were being shot by members of their own hunting party. Some hunters were also being shot by strangers. These cases all had one thing in common. The shooter was simply shooting at movement, which was indicative of a hunter who shot a turkey first and checked for a beard later. In the spring turkey season, only bearded birds are legal. These kinds of accidents supported wardens' arguments that a growing percentage of hunters shoot the first turkey they see, even if they haven't seen a beard on the bird.

The lack of responsibility by some of these hunters is alarming. After all, these people are firing a deadly weapon. There was a case in Vernon County in which a father had decided to take his young son along with him turkey hunting. They were the only people who had permission to hunt on the land so they felt safe there. As the two walked across an open hay field shortly before dawn, the young boy was shot in the face by a turkey hunter who was hidden in the brush next to the field. The man was trespassing as well.

When interviewed by the local warden the man claimed he thought the man and his son were turkeys. How can someone misidentify two people walking across a hay field as turkeys? Worse yet, how can such a man claim he saw a beard on the turkey before he shot? It is obvious what is going on in these cases. Some hunters shoot any turkey they see in the spring. If they walk up to the bird and find it is a hen, they either illegally strip the breast meat from it to take it home, or leave the hen to rot in the woods. The new turkey hunting tradition in Wisconsin deserves better than that.

Steven Dewald

Example of illegal turkey bait

20 Ethical Lapses

Some misbehavior in the outdoors cannot be addressed with a citation. It is not possible to enforce ethics. Over the course of my career there have been positive developments and negative developments as to how people interact with each other; as well as how they value our natural resources.

I am not a big fan of fishing tournaments. I like the smaller local tournaments organized by a local sportsman's club on a local lake. In these competitions, the prizes are modest and earnings from the contest go towards a local lake project. I like to support those events. However I am not wild about big money tournaments where the permit is held by an out-of-state organizer.

My biggest complaint with those tournaments is how tournament participants treat local fishermen. I have had many complaints over the years from people who were anchored in their favorite fishing spot when a tournament competitor roared in at high speed before throttling back; pushing a large wake into the anchored boat. The tournament angler throws a few casts adjacent to the other boat. After not catching anything, they roar away again causing disruption to the local angler both while they are coming and going. The perception, at least in the competitor's mind, is that his fishing is more important because he is competing for prize money.

There are also local sport fishermen who should care more about the resource. During the late winter months when the Mississippi River has the only open water available, some anglers will anchor in deep water to pull up sauger after sauger from 40 feet down. The fish come out of the water with their air bladders sticking out of the fish's mouth due to the rapid ascent from the depths. Most of the fish die, yet some of these anglers don't seem to care that they have killed three or four dozen fish in their afternoon of fishing.

This reminds me of walleye fishermen in the early 1980's prior to the statewide minimum 15 inch size limit. I would sometimes check these people with a limit of walleyes that all fit inside their minnow bucket. These people were keeping 5 fish, none of which were even a foot in length. The fish were still a year or two from reaching sexual maturity that would allow them to spawn. When I pointed this out to these fishermen, they would usually answer me sarcastically that there was no law against it so they were going to continue to keep the small game fish.

Deer hunters also could improve on how their sport is perceived. Each year as a warden, I would get complaints from concerned citizens about a hunter who would shoot a deer in November and would still have the deer hanging in a tree in early April. Besides the meat being spoiled, this kind of practice makes all hunters look bad.

Some deer hunters also push the envelope as to how they deal with the deer hunters on an adjoining property. Hunters have reported to me that a neighboring property owner drives his truck with the radio blaring, along their property line when they bow hunt in the fall. The offending neighbor apparently doesn't want them to kill any bucks before he can during the gun season. Another farmer spreads liquid manure on an easement road another group of hunters use to access their property on an easement road they paid for. There are also some hunters in Buffalo and Trempealeau County who hang strongly scented bars of soap on deer trails leading across the property boundary around their land. They apparently believe this will keep deer from leaving their land.

Other hunters try to privatize pieces of public land. There was a continuing problem in one of the counties I supervised where signs indicating access points to public hunting land were continually being ripped down. Hunters on neighboring properties didn't want outsiders to use public land they were trying to keep for themselves. The local warden finally got tired of repeatedly posting the signs so he did a news release in the county newspaper that described in great detail how people could use that parcel of land.

Every outdoor user needs to remember that how we use the outdoors affects other people. Rather than focusing on our own personal gain, we should do everything we can to enhance the experiences of the next generation of outdoor users.

The next generation

21 Earn-a-Buck or Earn a Fine

If you are a deer hunter in Wisconsin, you are well aware of a regulation called earn-a-buck. Under this rule, in specific management units hunters were required to first harvest an antlerless deer in order to earn the right to then harvest an antlered deer. The rule was first suggested by a state legislator which is a fact lost in deer hunting history.

The logic behind earn-a-buck was that too many hunters were only shooting bucks in overpopulated deer units. This is a trend that has become all too common over the past two decades. Many people have lost their historic connection with harvesting wild fish and game to supplement their family's diet. In the 1950's and 1960's, obtaining venison to eat had a much higher priority. The relentless media influence on harvesting trophy deer has persuaded younger generations of hunters that antlers are all that matters.

Without controlling the doe harvest in these units, the population could continue to rapidly expand leading to crop damage and the spread of disease. This was an especially important fact in the chronic wasting disease zone where deer populations in some areas were approaching a 100 deer per square mile, which is not sustainable.

Establishing a rule such as this one was not going to be popular. Hunters argued that this conflicted with their hunting traditions. That is true, but then chronic wasting disease is not part of our hunting traditions either. The disease is now present and we would be irresponsible in our commitment to future generations of Wisconsin hunters if we chose to simply allow the disease to spread. There are numerous western states that now feel they should have been more aggressive in slowing the spread of the disease in their states. They now have to deal with deer populations that have dropped significantly as chronic wasting disease infection rates reach 40% or more of the deer population.

Enforcing the earn-a-buck regulations led to new challenges for wardens. We soon learned that some hunters would do everything possible to get around the law. Some hunters attempted to register a doe multiple times at a deer registration station to obtain multiple earn-a-buck stickers that enabled multiple hunters to then register a buck. The hunting parties would leave the registration station with a registered doe and one buck sticker. They would then cut off the registration tag from the doe and send another member of the party to register the doe again to get another buck sticker. The DNR then had to require registration attendants in earn-a-buck zones to cut off one ear of each antlerless deer so the deer could not be registered multiple times.

Lowly car-killed deer suddenly became a prized possession. Some hunters would grab a dead doe on the side of the road to claim it as a deer they had shot to earn a buck sticker. The DNR then had to issue cans of blaze orange spray paint to county Sheriff's departments so that the deputy could spray paint on the car-killed deer at the accident scene to show it was not killed by a hunter.

Out in the deer woods the situation was also challenging, especially on opening weekend of the deer gun season. Some hunters were ethical and passed on a buck the first hour of the season. There were many others who would not. I was working with Richard, the warden in Vernon County during the 2004 deer gun season, when we received a phone call the second day of the season. The complainant advised that there were several hunters on a property who had been shooting every buck that ran past them on opening day. The complainant had been doing the ethical thing, passing on bucks until he had harvested a doe. He was frustrated that each time he would hold his fire on a buck passing by his deer stand; shots would be heard as soon as the bucks crossed on to the neighboring property.

This was taking place near Avalanche, a small village that isn't much more than an intersection of two roads with a small grocery store. It is an area with steep oak ridges accented by trout streams below. We arrived near the property late in the day to wait for hunters to return to camp. I was dropped off on foot down the road to observe the camp from a distance. When I observed hunters returning to camp, I radioed Richard to pick me up. We then drove to the cabin and found three hunters outside.

Naturally the men were surprised to see that we were game wardens. We started the contact with a check of licenses to make it look like a routine check. This is usually a good tactic since it gives wardens time to evaluate how nervous hunters are before moving forward with the investigation. The men were not all that at ease when we asked them simple questions such as whether or not they had shot any deer yet.

We then informed the men this was not a routine visit. We told the men we were there to investigate the bucks they had shot. Each of us took one of the hunters aside to interview them separately so they could not organize an alibi together. It didn't take long before we were making progress. Richard determined one of the hunters had only hunted here briefly and was not involved with the shooting of the deer. That hunter was allowed to leave.

The hunter I interviewed admitted to shooting a buck opening day. When I asked where it was now, he informed me it was still on the ridge hidden under some leaves. I told the hunter to take me there. The man had been using an ATV to go up and down the very high ridge above us. He told me I could ride on the back as he drove up the steep logging road. When we reached the top of the ridge he led me to an 8 point buck half covered under oak leaves. The buck had been gutted but was not tagged. The buck's body was stiff indicating it had been shot the day before.

We loaded the buck on to the back of the ATV to take it down the ridge to our vehicles. The man said there wasn't room for me to sit on the ATV if he was going to haul the buck down on the back of the machine. I told the hunter that would not be a problem. The man drove down the road back to the camp 600 yards below. Rather than leave the man get out of sight with the evidence, I simply jogged down the road behind him.

When the man got to the cabin with the deer, he turned off the ATV and got off the machine. When he turned around and saw me standing there, he did a double take. He looked at me, then looked up the ridge, then looked at me again. He couldn't quite believe that I was the same warden he left on the ridge. He finally asked, "How did you get here?" I simply answered that I jogged down the road behind him. The man was apparently one of those hunters who only hunted where his ATV would take him. He couldn't believe I had jogged that far. I told the man that jogging downhill wasn't much of a challenge. I then added that the other warden could have probably done that running uphill.

When Richard looked in the bed of the truck parked next to the cabin, he saw freshly wrapped packages of meat. This suggested that someone had butchered a deer or two and had left the packages in the back of the truck to freeze overnight in the night air. After discovering the packages of meat, Richard had been successful in obtaining the truth from the other hunter. The man admitted that there were three bucks shot opening day including an 8 point buck, a 5 point buck, and a spike buck. The man stated he and his partner had butchered two bucks and had dumped the remains in a ravine west of the cabin. I then agreed to take photos of the butchered carcasses in the ravine while Richard finished taking statements from both men. The men were subsequently charged for taking multiple illegal deer and lost their hunting privileges.

The earn-a-buck rule was eliminated after I retired from the warden service. It remains to be seen if another tool to control the spread of chronic wasting disease in Wisconsin will be developed or if political leaders will simply allow the disease to spread statewide.

Steven Dewald

Buck hidden under leaves during earn-a-buck season

22 Digging Ginseng

You could call ginseng the money root. It is a very valuable natural resource in Wisconsin. Dried ginseng root sells for more than $350 a pound most seasons. The Chinese in particular value Wisconsin wild ginseng. They believe it to be more potent than domestically grown root cultivated on ginseng farms, which is why wild root is much more expensive per pound.

Monitoring the harvest of wild ginseng takes wardens into a shadowy world. There are legal and ethical ginseng diggers. However it is also painfully obvious that a large percentage of ginseng harvesters are both trespassers and thieves. Ginseng is protected on all state lands such as wildlife areas, state forests, state parks, and public hunting grounds. Therefore the only place to legally dig ginseng is on private land.

Wardens monitor public lands in western Wisconsin where ginseng commonly grows. Each year arrests are made of people illegally digging the root on public land. Although the ginseng season does not begin until September 1st each year, ginseng poachers are active most of the summer. Catching a ginseng poacher in the act is not easy. These people usually are dressed in full camouflage to blend in with the summer foliage. The smarter poachers do not leave a vehicle parked in the area. They are instead dropped off by an accomplice who only returns to the area when the poacher calls them back with a cell phone call.

In recent years, with the popularity of trail cameras, landowners are finally beginning to realize how much ginseng poaching is taking place in rural areas. As more cameras are placed on forest trails, more and more ginseng poachers are turning up in trail camera photos. The majority of landowners don't realize the financial hit they are taking when their ginseng is illegally harvested from the family farm. However a few knowledgeable landowners who encourage ginseng growth on their land are all too aware of what they have lost when they find their ginseng patch destroyed a month before the season. Thefts of well tended patches can cost more than a thousand dollars in lost revenue to the landowner. Ginseng is not a fast growing crop. It may take a decade to produce large quality roots.

The high value of the root has led to a decreasing wild ginseng resource. Overharvest is eliminating the plants from many areas. Although ginseng regulations have been changed to encourage harvest of only mature plants, most ginseng poachers will take whatever they can find. That is why ginseng poachers are often cited for not carrying the ginseng plant stems with them when checked in the field.

By requiring ginseng harvesters to carry the stems, the warden can determine how many prongs grow from the stem of the plant which indicates whether the plant is mature or not. Most poachers don't even try to comply since they don't care about replanting seed or only harvesting mature plants. After all they are simple thieves; trying to quickly steal whatever valuables they can get away with from a private landowner's forest.

One additional check and balance to the ginseng harvest system is the ginseng buyer. These buyers are required to have their ginseng certified as legal ginseng before exporting the root overseas. The buyer is also required to maintain buyer records of the seller name and pounds of root sold. It is important that the ginseng buyer is also legal and ethical. If they are not, they sometimes buy large quantities of root from ginseng poachers the first day of the season without asking any questions. A ginseng poacher selling 12 pounds of root on opening day of the season has obviously been digging most of the summer. Yet some buyers look the other way to also get in on the action. Selling the root is lucrative at both the retail and wholesale level. As with other high value natural resources in Wisconsin, the temptation of easy money causes some ginseng harvesters to leave their ethics at home.

23 Migrant Hunters

It was early November in 2010. I was working in Vernon County where I was spending an evening with Dale working night enforcement. Early November is usually the peak of the rut when poachers are very active trying to harvest trophy bucks. Our initial plans for the evening were put on hold when we received a radio call from the Sheriff's department that they had a complaint of shining and shots fired on a farm in the western part of the county. A deputy was already in the area and had observed spotlights working on the farm.

The farm was an organic farm that produced vegetables in large quantities. The landowner had a permit to harvest deer under an agricultural damage permit. However night hunting is not allowed under these permits due to safety concerns. One of the primary rules of firearm safety is to be sure of your target and beyond. However if someone shoots at a deer illuminated in a beam from a spotlight, what lies beyond the deer is invisible in the darkness. A person or home could be in the background behind the deer that would not be visible after dark.

We followed the deputy into the farm yard with our warden truck. There was no activity visible when we left our vehicles. The deputy went back on to the county highway to check for illegal activity around the area. Dale and I began to walk around in the dark to look behind the farm buildings to determine if we could see or hear any illegal activity. We were several hundred yards behind the buildings when we saw a vehicle stop on the county road several hundred more yards away. Two people from the vehicle then ran up the hill into the woods carrying a flashlight. We didn't have a clear view of them but it appeared they may have retrieved a raccoon or deer from the hillside. Yet that was totally separate activity from what we were investigating since the deputy was sure the spotlight had been used on the farm we were on.

Not seeing or hearing any sign of poachers, we came to the conclusion that the suspects were probably hiding in the woods until after we left. We talked about our options until I suggested that we make a noisy departure from the farm. I told Dale to slam his truck door twice and to then drive out of the driveway. While he was doing that, I was going to quietly slip into a cornfield on the other side of the driveway where I could watch the door to the house. I had hoped that the poachers would eventually sneak back to the house if that is where they had originated from.

Patience is an important trait if you intend to be a successful game warden. There are hundreds of situations in a year's time, where a warden has to evaluate if waiting is the best strategy. In this case it was. After approximately a half hour, I observed two men to walk out of the darkness to enter the home. I then radioed to Dale what I had observed. He drove up to the house a few minutes later. We then knocked on the door and made contact with the men inside.

We found the people living in the house to be migrant workers from Mexico. They worked on the farm during the entire growing season. We discussed hunting deer with them. Although language was somewhat of a barrier, one man spoke enough English to clarify that the landowner had told them they could shoot deer when they were in the vegetables. We explained to the men that the landowner did have a deer damage permit but that did not allow hunting of deer at night.

We eventually decided to issue a citation for a lesser charge instead of a criminal charge of shining deer with a firearm. The men were in violation of the more serious law. However we took into consideration the fact that they were migrant workers from Mexico, who relied on their employer to instruct them in how to follow the terms of the shooting permit. We then left the men and the farm. Dale also made contact with the landowner in subsequent days. He explained what had taken place and suggested what training should be given to migrant workers in the future to avoid repeating the incident.

24 Littering: Every Little Bit Hurts

During my career as a warden I was always amazed that people could carry full cans of pop and beer down to a stream to fish, but could not find the energy to carry the lighter empty cans back to their vehicle. Litter along our lakes and streams where people fish is a significant problem throughout the state.

Some people leave large snarls of monofilament line on the shorelines that snare and kill wildlife. Pop and beer cans, bait containers, foam coffee cups, and fast food bags litter the shorelines. There are also problems with litter left behind by hunters. In many counties dozens of complaints are phoned in to wardens after the deer gun season as hunters dump boned-out carcasses from deer in road ditches. In some deer management units, headless bucks are also found. Some hunters remove the head and cape of their trophy deer and leave the very edible meat to rot. Apparently finding a family interested in using the meat takes too much effort.

Moving day for people renting homes and apartments can also pose litter problems. Wardens often get calls from concerned citizens who report finding piles of household goods in a roadside ravine. When wardens investigate, they usually find that someone dumped the pile of debris when they had to vacate a rental property. Sometimes the debris includes appliances that people are too cheap to pay a $15 recycling fee on.

The cumulative effect of thoughtless acts committed hundreds of times a year is depressing. Wardens have tried to address the issue by organizing citizen cleanups of local rivers as community projects. In some areas of the state, cumulative tonnage of litter and debris recovered from a single river is in the tens of thousands of pounds. Industrial size dumpsters at these cleanup points often include tires, barrels of unknown substances, car batteries, parts of cars, and chemical containers.

It is hard to understand why some people have such little regard for our environment. However as a warden I also saw how some people live in their homes. Once I experienced visiting homes that were totally trashed, it wasn't so hard to understand why the same people felt comfortable trashing the outdoors.

I remember a trip I made to visit a woman in rural Jefferson County. I was asked to talk to her because people using the new DNR bike trail were complaining that she was using the DNR easement as a grazing area for her goats. When I drove into the woman's yard, I saw a fair amount of debris around the home. As I started to walk to the house, I heard a grunt from a station wagon parked outside. I saw some movement in the back of the wagon that did not appear to be human. When I took a few steps closer, I discovered a half grown pig in the cargo area of the wagon. The station wagon was apparently being used as a mobile hog house! I would hate to buy that car off the used car lot.

Alcohol often plays a role in littering. I was working with another warden during Riverfest over the 4th of July weekend in LaCrosse when we observed a group of people drinking beer on a sand bar. They didn't have any camping equipment with them, so we assumed this was just a temporary party spot. We hoped we would not have to wait long before the group left. Leaving the scene without picking up the numerous beer cans was the critical element in the case.

Fortunately it took less than an hour for the group to leave. As we suspected, they made no effort to pick up their trash. As they left the shore in a boat, we made contact with them. We cited several individuals in the group for leaving behind 23 beer cans. The case also took an interesting turn when we found that one of the men had an outstanding warrant for $8000 for failure to pay child support. We were happy that justice was served in more ways than one.

Some littering investigations turn up an amount of litter that is much more significant than a few dozen beer cans. My first year as a warden I discovered two very large piles of garbage on the banks of the Fox River near Waukesha. As I dug through the garbage it was apparent that the waste was coming from two nearby residences. During the course of the investigation I determined that the two families had been using the river bank as their personal dump for 5 years and 15 years respectively. When spring floods came along, the garbage was conveniently washed away from the bank of the river. Both families were cited and were required to truck away the remaining garbage.

Probably the strangest littering arrest I was ever involved with began with a 911 call in Crawford County. I was spending the day on boat patrol with Mike, the warden from Prairie du Chien. The Sheriff's department dispatcher called us to respond to a 911 call for help from a pontoon boat in a slough north of Prairie du Chien. The caller advised they needed officers to respond due to the fact the operator of the boat was intoxicated and the other passengers feared for their safety. It was the only time in my career when we received a call from a passenger about a boat operator on the same boat.

We immediately responded to the scene. When we found the pontoon boat, the passengers waved us over to talk to them. The operator of the pontoon was not thrilled to see us. We were very surprised to discover that everyone on the boat was from the same family. The father was the man driving the boat. Apparently they were trying to get him to take them home but he refused.

When we began to talk to the man we soon learned why they were afraid. The man was very uncooperative and agitated. He obviously did not like law enforcement officers. The operator stated that if we wanted to arrest him, then we should arrest him as he held his clenched fists forward. The man stated he only had one beer and we did not see any evidence that suggested otherwise. In fact, the man was quickly drinking one can of pop after another in rapid succession.

We had to be quite firm with him to follow us down the slough back to town. The man was angry with us and was acting hyperactive. His movements were jerky and unpredictable. We began to suspect the man had mental problems. The man's wife, who was a passenger on the boat, finally took over the controls and began to steer the boat to follow us down the slough. The man continued to yell at her and to point down other sloughs trying to get her to steer away from our path of travel.

It was also unexpected when the man tossed his pop can into the water in plain view from our boat. It appeared to be an act of defiance. We turned the patrol boat around and retrieved the floating can on the water as evidence. I then began writing a citation to the man for littering which was completed by the time we arrived at the man's dock. A City of Prairie du Chien police officer was also standing by at the man's residence. We learned later that the man had posted a sign on his front door of his home warning he would shoot any police officers who bothered him. The police department already knew this but we did not.

We presented the man with his citation for littering. The man responded by crumpling it in his hands and then told us he was going to throw it in the river. His wife yelled at him not to do so. He finally walked from the boat to his house with the citation still in hand. The rest of the man's family thanked us for responding to their call. We then left to continue our patrol, hoping we had dealt with our last mentally unstable man for the day.

25 Poachers Pay in Unusual Ways

In the first week of November of 2000, I was investigating complaints of illegal dumping of deer carcasses in LaCrosse County. Normally this is a problem that takes place after the deer gun season is over. However, the complainant in this case advised there were multiple deer dumped on Swamp road with some of the deer nearly intact. Since the call had been made to the Sheriff's department, a deputy asked me if I could assist him at the scene which I was happy to do.

We found three distinct locations where deer had been dumped. At the first location, there were three deer carcasses thrown into the road ditch. One of the carcasses still had the hunter's deer tag attached which obviously was a serious strategic error for the man who had dumped the carcasses. The second location had one carcass that appeared to be present for a month or more and was badly decomposed with no evidence of the owner.

The third location had a very fresh carcass of a buck deer with the head and cape removed. The meat appeared to be fresh and was not spoiled. Whoever had dumped the buck only wanted the head and cape. It bothered me to see that someone had such little respect for this animal. The buck had a very large body and likely also had a large set of antlers. It deserved more respect than this.

The deputy and I decided to split the investigative duties. He agreed to take the hunter's deer tag to track down the responsible party for the first littering event. Meanwhile I chose to visit local taxidermists in the area to see if I could determine if my suspect had dropped off a buck for mounting. I had hoped I could match a cape with the carcass along the road.

While in one taxidermist's place of business, the owner advised he had just received a head and cape from a man who stated he had shot the buck near Barre Mills. This was the area the carcass had been found. The taxidermist had more than enough deer to work on so this head and cape was in his freezer and had not been worked on yet. When we examined the cape, we found an obvious slug hole in the hide. This was significant because the deer gun season did not open for another two weeks. I then seized the head and cape as evidence. However when I later took the cape to the littering scene I found that it did not match the remaining portions of the hide left on the deer. In other words, I now had two cases to investigate rather than one.

I went to the residence of the man who had dropped off the buck at the taxidermist. I asked the man to come outside where I had the cape in the back of my truck. The man had an injury to his head near his ear with bruising and some form of antiseptic applied to the skin. I didn't ask the man about his medical condition. I then showed the man the slug hole in the cape and explained that it was obvious this deer had been shot with a shotgun. The man denied this and retrieved a hunting arrow from his vehicle and stated that was the arrow he had shot it with.

I took the arrow and placed the entire broad head arrow tip within the slug hole without touching the sides. I again advised the man it was obviously a slug hole. I decided to take the man to a confession in steps rather than all at once. I told the man I did not know why he had tagged a deer that was obviously shot with a gun. I asked if he had found the deer dead and had just tagged it.

The man quickly admitted that was the case. He told me where he had been hunting near Barre Mills and that after hearing a gunshot, he watched the buck run into some thick cover and die. He stated that his ego got the best of him and that he tagged it because he thought it would be a Pope and Young buck. (Pope and Young is an organization that recognizes trophy bucks taken with bow and arrow.) I always marveled that people could take such pride in a mount that wasn't legally taken.

I told the man this was illegal. I asked the man if he had to do anything to the buck to finish it off and the man stated that no, it was already dead when he got to it. I then asked the man where the meat was. He did not want to answer at first but finally advised me the meat was at a meat processor in Cashton. I then told the man the meat would be seized and a citation for possession of a gunshot deer tagged with an archery tag would come later.

After I left the man's home, I called the warden in Vernon County and asked him to pay a visit to the meat processor to see what the story was on that end. When the warden and his recruit seized the meat, the processor advised that the suspect had told him he shot it with an arrow and that he had fallen out of the tree stand after he shot the deer. The meat processor also advised the buck was obviously shot with a gun because the ribs were shattered. Another informant also advised us the next day that the man had broken his shotgun when he fell from the tree.

A few days later I went to the suspect's home to interview the man again. When I arrived at his residence I asked him if his shotgun had been fixed yet. The man stated that it was and then realized I knew more about what had taken place. I put the shotgun in the back of my truck and told the man we knew he had shot the buck with his shotgun. I looked at him and told him that I guessed his head injury was from the shotgun hitting his head when he hit the ground. The man advised that was true. He stated the barrel had hit him near his ear and that he was knocked out from the fall out of the tree. The man could not explain why he poached the deer. He knew what he did was wrong. Now he was facing a criminal charge for an illegal deer with a mandatory 3 years of lost DNR privileges. The man was also nearly killed when he fell from a high tree stand to the ground with a loaded shotgun. He learned the hard way that poaching can be dangerous.

In another incident in LaCrosse County, a hunter learned that illegal activities can generate a painful lesson delivered by another hunter. In this case, a man with no common sense began firing his weapon at several deer running across a county highway. He continued to shoot at the deer on the other side of the road even as a vehicle crossed into the line of fire. The driver saw what was taking place and hit the brakes, skidding to a stop. However he did not drive on when the shooting stopped. He instead put the car in park and went directly to the man who had fired the dangerous shots. The physically strong driver of the car then delivered a well-thrown punch to the shooter's face, dropping him with one punch. As they say, crime doesn't pay.

26 Mussel Men

The Mississippi River is home to a variety of fresh water mussels or clams. Native Americans used the clams. In the late 1800's, before the days of plastic, clam shell button factories were common in towns along the big river. The clam shells were cut and drilled into buttons that held up well to the demands of clothing manufacturers. In those early days, clams were usually collected with brail bars which were heavy bars pulled over the clam beds from a boat above. The bars had small metal hooks on them that the clam would close on, as the hook passed in to the open shell. In very shallow water there were also clam divers, who would dive to the bottom while holding their breath to grab a few clams before re-surfacing.

There wasn't a lot of demand for clams in recent times until the Japanese pearl industry made a discovery. The pearl industry was always looking for ways to mass produce near perfect pearls. One day they discovered that by cutting out a small circle from a Mississippi River clam shell and placing it into a domestic mussel, the mussel would form a very valuable pearl around the piece of shell. The clam shells from the Mississippi were of a particular thickness that made this possible.

Soon several commercial mussel species from Wisconsin including Three Ridge and Washboard clams were in high demand. It was to be a typical boom and bust type natural resource story. In the years around 1990, it seemed like every river rat in western Wisconsin had discovered clamming. Harvesting shell did not require a college education or a lot of equipment. A flat-bottomed boat, some scuba gear and an air compressor was all that was needed. Many clammers soon realized how lucrative it could be. At the peak of the clam shell demand in the mid-1990's, some local clammers were harvesting up to a thousand dollars of clams per day! A few local men were taking in more money than they had seen their entire life. Almost overnight, poor river boys were driving around in brand new pickup trucks. It was like a modern day gold rush. Some of the larger washboard clams were selling for $4-5 per clam.

When you have that kind of money flowing into a natural resource, law enforcement challenges inevitably develop. Wardens working on the Mississippi River were then thrust into the middle of the clamming boom while still having to address all of their other regular duties. No additional wardens were stationed on the Mississippi River just because a new industry was created.

Clamming took place in open water months on the river when divers in scuba gear would dive to the bottom with heavy weighted belts. Then by feel, due to the turbidity of the water, they would move their hands over the bottom of the river, sliding clams into mesh sacks. When the sack was full, a clam tender in the boat would pull up the heavy sack and would attempt to push the individual clam shells through metal rings to see which clams had reached the minimum legal diameter in size. At least that is the way it was supposed to work.

With a bag of clams worth hundreds of dollars, even undersize clams were kept by some clammers. The shadier operators would hide the bags of undersize shell on river islands, in shallow water near boat landings, or would sink them with a marker to be collected later. Wardens working clammers soon realized it was a hot and dirty job. Peak clamming activity took place in the hot summer months. There were many hours of surveillance that needed to be conducted from mosquito infested river islands in the hot summer sun. This was followed with inspections of the clam shells in which many bags of muddy clam shells had to be measured one shell at a time.

Some clam buyers contributed to the illegal harvest problem by buying sub-legal shell or by purchasing protected species of mussels taken illegally from inland waters of Wisconsin. When natural resource staff from Upper Mississippi River states met to discuss the clamming industry trends, industry shell buyers with diamond studded rings and other fancy jewelry would show up at these interstate conferences to see what regulators might be planning next. The larger buyers, who also acted as exporters to Japan, had become rich overnight.

As the clamming beds on the middle stretches of the Mississippi River were cleaned out by overharvest, clammers worked their way north into Iowa and Wisconsin. Soon clammers with southern accents and names like "Billy Bob" were claiming a post office box address and establishing residency in places like Prairie du Chien.

Dennis, the warden in Prairie du Chien at the time, recognized the need to communicate between officers in other river states as to what was going on and who all the players were. Some of the clammers were trying to purchase resident licenses in multiple states. Others had outstanding warrants for clamming violations farther down river. Some clammers had also demonstrated that they could be violent with conservation wardens when contacted so there was an obvious need to share that information with other officers. To respond to these concerns, Dennis created the "Clam Cop" newsletter which was a law enforcement summary electronically distributed several times a month to wardens in a half dozen states along the Mississippi River.

The U.S. Fish and Wildlife Service also needed to be involved to deal with the interstate transportation of illegally harvested clam shell. This is a violation of the Lacey Act which makes it a federal violation to transport any illegally harvested natural resources across state lines. These agents also began to work on investigating the clam buyers.

By 1998, the boom changed to bust. A local clam buyer in Wisconsin paid a $35000 penalty for purchasing illegal shell from inland Wisconsin waters. A large Midwestern clam buyer had $300,000 worth of clam shell seized from him that led to time in Federal prison and a corresponding high financial penalty. By this time the Wisconsin clam population was also severely depleted both by overharvest and the emergence of the invasive zebra mussel population. The final nail in the clamming coffin was a disease outbreak in the Japanese cultured pearl industry that killed demand for the Wisconsin shell. All clam shelling seasons in Wisconsin are now closed with the hope that someday the resource may recover.

27 Unusual Reactions

If there is one thing all law enforcement officers quickly learn, it is that they need to be prepared for anything during their work. Not all people react in a reasonable or logical manner. Some people have truly weird responses to events that take place.

One of the first hunting accident investigations I was involved with took place in Jefferson County during the deer gun season. It involved a group of 8 people who decided to conduct a deer drive that was doomed from the very start. The group placed 4 standers and an equal number of drivers at opposite ends of a 150 yard long grass field. The grass had only grown to a height of three feet, so all of the hunters were visible to each other at all times.

With nothing between the two lines of people, the drivers then began to march forward towards the standers they were facing. A large buck jumped up between the two groups and began to run off between the two lines of hunters. In a moment of mass stupidity, both lines of hunters opened fire as the deer ran between the two lines. The buck escaped unharmed, but a woman in the group went down with the first volley of rounds from the shotguns. She took a 12 gauge shotgun slug in her hip which caused her to immediately drop to the ground.

A county deputy and I responded to the call. When we arrived on scene, the woman was beginning to get medical attention from first responders. As I began to talk with her, one of the first things she told me was that she did not want to cooperate because she didn't want to press charges against anyone. She instead said to us, "Just give me a cigarette." I was surprised that someone would react that way but as I interviewed the rest of the group they didn't appear to think this was such a big deal. They also thought their plan to drive this grassy patch was a sound one. The man I interviewed who I believed to be the shooter stated that he didn't think a shotgun slug went that far. I responded that obviously it did.

I was even more troubled by another hunting accident that took place during one summer in Jefferson County. A retired man was entertaining relatives including his grandchildren at his home. While the relatives were in and around the home, he spotted a starling on his bird feeder. He reached for his 22 caliber rifle and slowly slid the end of the barrel through a crack in his patio door. He unfortunately pulled the trigger at the exact second that his granddaughter passed in front of the patio door while she ran around the house. The bullet struck her in the temple killing her instantly. It was a terrible tragedy.

DNR headquarters clarified for me that since the man was shooting at a bird it was considered to be a hunting accident; which explained my involvement. Several deputies and I collected information about the incident and the firearm. It is customary for the local District Attorney's office to review reports of these fatalities before evidence is returned. Just a few days after the fatality, the shooter called me on the phone at my home extremely angry. He demanded to know why I had not yet returned the rifle to him. I was shocked that he would have this perspective, considering it would be constant reminder of his granddaughter's death. I guess that isn't the way he looked at the situation.

A retired warden shared with me an experience he had in Clark County when he was a field warden there. He received a call about an elderly man who had been killed in a hunting accident during the deer gun season. When he arrived at the scene, he found the victim dead on the ground but no one else was there. A half hour later, as family members returned to the scene, he learned that after their grandfather was found to be deceased, the rest of the hunting group continued the deer drive. They left the scene in pursuit of the same buck they had shot at that led to the death of their family member.

One hunting accident that I am thankful never happened was actually a planned event in Jefferson County. A local woman was having an affair with a co-worker. They wanted to be together but because the woman had a husband, the marriage was complicating the matter. The woman asked her lover to take her husband deer hunting and to kill him in the woods and claim it was a hunting accident. The boyfriend took the man out hunting several days in a row. However each time he was about to do the deadly deed, another hunter would walk into view. The man and woman eventually changed plans and shot the husband at home while making it appear a burglary had taken place.

The details of the plan were made known to investigators when the boyfriend called his landlord on the phone and told him that he should hide a tape from the tape recorder near the phone so police would not hear it. The landlord naturally made sure that was the first thing the police obtained. The boyfriend apparently had some doubts about how committed the woman was to him, so he had taped all of the conversations between them recording how they planned to kill the husband.

For the rest of my warden career that case was always in the back of my mind when I responded to hunting accidents. I was always conscious of the fact that the next accident call may very well be a homicide. I also remembered that distraught family members could instead be very good actors. Fortunately, such a situation never came up in the cases I responded to. However homicides in the woods have taken place during deer season in other areas of the state.

28 They Stole our College Fund!

On a snowy day in January of 1996, I received a call from a very upset landowner. He was calling to report a timber theft on his land in LaCrosse County. Timber theft is unfortunately a fairly common occurrence in western Wisconsin. The very valuable red oak and black walnut trees in the area sometimes tempt dishonest people. They try to get some extra money during their own timber sale by sneaking additional trees from a neighboring property.

The landowner complainant advised that a logging truck was at a field where his logs had been skidded to and he was worried that his logs would leave before a law enforcement officer could respond. Another warden and I prepared to quickly leave the office to drive to the site. We first made a phone call to the county conservation office to ask if any county cutting notices had been issued in the area. They advised they had issued a permit on a neighboring property. County cutting permits are required to ensure that lands enrolled in the Managed Forest Law are current on their property tax payments before a harvest is begun. Some counties in the hill country such as LaCrosse County also require the permits to ensure logging roads are completed in an environmentally sound manner on the steep slopes.

When we arrived at the scene, we found two logging employees who were finishing loading logs on to two semi-trucks. The men told the wardens they had heard about the timber theft but that they were taking their logs from a different property. They advised another log skidder operator had just appeared in the area in recent days that was not associated with their operation. After their information was written down, the men were then allowed to leave.

The landowner who had made the complaint then came out to the field to speak with us. He told us that he had been keeping some older red oak trees in his forest in anticipation of the day when his children would go to college. The trees were his college fund. He was very upset that someone would go on to his land and cut the trees without his permission. The man then led us to his property and pointed out his southern fence line where a log skidder had crossed to remove trees from his land.

We followed the skid trails back to the field and counted 108 8-foot logs. Many of the logs appeared to be of veneer quality and were up to 24 inches in diameter. This was a very valuable stack of logs. I then phoned the landowners who had filed the cutting permit with the county. I asked to meet with them. They advised I could meet them at their home.

I met with the neighboring property owners and found them to be an elderly couple. I took out a plat book and an aerial photo and asked if they could show me where their land was. They accurately pointed out that they owned the land south of the fence line the complainant had showed to me. I then showed them where the logs had been taken without permission from their neighbor's property. The husband and wife were angry with the suggestion and were not apologetic. However they also added that they were too old to walk property lines and had instead told another neighbor to show the logger where to go. The third neighbor was the landowner who had hired the other logging company.

Like other investigations I had been on, this one was becoming increasingly complicated. I met with the other warden who had made contact by phone with the second logging company, which owned the other skidder. The second logger arrived at the scene and stated he had cut the logs in question earlier in the week. He then informed us that the third neighbor had told him that everything north of the fence line in question belonged to the elderly couple instead of everything south of the line. We began to believe that the third neighbor may have been trying to get paid for logs from the elderly couple's property but were unable to prove that enough to prosecute the man. The third neighbor had denied this.

The offending logger felt bad about the whole situation. He told us that when a landowner tells him where his property fence is, he has to believe the guy. Unfortunately, this particular landowner was not truthful. The logger understood he would have to pay the victim landowner for the logs. In fact, if the landowner wanted to file a civil action in court, under Wisconsin law he was entitled to double stumpage or twice the value of the logs. However in the end no one was happy. Several neighbors left knowing they could no longer trust their other neighbors. None of it would have happened if the third neighbor had been an honest man.

Like many situations in a warden's career, this case involved a significant amount of conflict resolution between various people. We wanted to provide some justice to the victim. However, the future plans for his timber were now gone forever. He would now have to accept the payment for the logs along with the corresponding unscheduled income tax hit for this year. He would also have to develop another strategy for his children's college fund.

29 The Egg Men

When I worked on the Mississippi River in the 1990's, the most valuable commercial fish at the time was catfish. Commercial fishermen were still quite active when I arrived in LaCrosse. In fact there were still fish buying stations in various river towns including LaCrosse. Some commercial fisherman would put out a gill net or set line just to earn some "beer money." However the more serious commercial operators would fish full time at various times of the year for sheephead or drum, carp, buffalo, and catfish.

These fish were not selling for a lot of money per pound. It was common to sell carp at 8 cents a pound, sheephead at 12 cents, and catfish at 45 cents a pound. The catfish were vulnerable to winter seine hauls. A seine is a large fabric of net that forms an underwater bag or pouch as it is pulled through the water under the ice. If the commercial fisherman can find a catfish wintering hole, many thousands of pounds of catfish can be seined in one haul.

However fish managers recognized that catfish can lie dormant in these wintering holes, so they enacted a rule in the commercial fishing code that only allowed commercial fishermen to take up to 100 pounds of catfish per seine haul. Some people would attempt to get around the rule by sneaking out to their seine of bagged fish at night to smuggle out a couple hundred extra pounds of catfish. A few also tried to cover their tracks via false paperwork.

We had one commercial fisherman who was found to be selling unusually priced rough fish to an out-of-state fish buyer. A commercial fishing records audit conducted by wardens along the river found that the man was submitting catch reports and sale receipts for carp and sheephead, but was getting paid in amounts that indicated catfish. When the investigation was completed the man was convicted of a Lacey Act violation in Federal court for transporting illegally obtained fish or game across state lines. The man had falsified records to conceal the catfish sales.

What we didn't know then was that commercial fishing was about to follow a new, more profitable path. In the year 2001, the sale of shovelnose sturgeon on the Upper Mississippi River nearly doubled from the year before. These sturgeon were not being pursued as much for meat as for their roe or eggs. Wardens were about to learn that the "egg men" would soon add a new responsibility to their workload.

Russia had been the world's leading supplier of caviar prior to this. However with the fall of the Soviet Union, there was much less government control of the sturgeon harvest there. In fact, from all appearances the Russian Mafia had taken over control of the resource. Overharvest of the Russian sturgeon led to a population collapse. It was reported that the roe harvest from Beluga caviar crashed by 85% in just one year. Due to the lucrative caviar market worldwide, roe buyers had to find new sources of caviar. One couple in Indiana made sales of $600,000 worth of paddlefish roe in 2001. Paddlefish are protected in Wisconsin but can be harvested in a few southern states. By 2002 Russian caviar buyers were appearing in Wisconsin. Some were cited for wholesale fish buying violations.

Lake sturgeon are not allowed to be harvested by commercial fishermen in Wisconsin. However, shovelnose sturgeon are allowed to be taken commercially on the Mississippi River. Although smaller than a lake sturgeon, a female shovelnose sturgeon full of eggs is still worth $50 a piece. Similar to what happened in the clamming boom and bust cycle, the sturgeon and paddlefish populations in the middle states of the Mississippi

River are now under tremendous harvest pressure. This is pushing demand for roe north into Wisconsin waters.

One surprising development in the pursuit of new roe sources is that dogfish roe is now being sought. The dogfish is about the least respected fish on the Mississippi River. However, now even dogfish roe can be sold at a good price. Not all species have roe that is fit for sale. Roe from a fish called a gar is actually toxic if ingested.

If the demand for roe follows the same path as the demand for clams on the Mississippi River, one could expect that southern roe harvesters will eventually find their way into Wisconsin waters. The demand for caviar is not slowing down while the supply is declining. Wardens fear that in the next decade, the caviar trade will pose significant challenges to commercial fishing enforcement on the Mississippi River. Wardens are already receiving reports of dead paddlefish with slit bellies floating in Lake Pepin. Hook and line fishermen may also begin to see paddlefish and lake sturgeon poachers snagging fish below the river's lock and dams.

30 The Things People Say

When you deal with thousands of different people every year, you learn to accept the fact that some people are not honest. When people are violating the law, they often will tell a tall tale that has only hints of the truth in the story. However it is disappointing that these people also lie in court while under oath.

I was working the largest ice fishing tournament of the year on Lake Koshkonong in Jefferson County when I entered an ice fishing shack to check the licenses of the occupants. The two men had 7 lines in the water including one extra tip-up. They at first denied the extra tip-up was theirs but evidence in the snow showed their footprints were the only ones that walked back and forth to the extra device. When I informed the men that they were over their legal limit of lines, I asked the men who was going to accept responsibility for the extra line. One man answered that I should give the citation to him. I seized the extra tip-up in question as evidence after the citation was issued.

Fishing with too many lines isn't the crime of the century and I very rarely had a court trial on such matters. However this man was different. He requested a court trial before the judge. The judge was also a unique character, well-known in the county for the somewhat abrasive style he exhibited to courtroom staff and law enforcement officers. In fact at one point some courthouse employees even filed a complaint against him with a judicial review board. Needless to say, I was never eager to have a trial in front of this particular judge.

The testimony in the "too many lines" case went fairly quick. I gave my testimony of what I had observed and what the man had told me when I asked who was going to take responsibility for the violation. When the man gave his testimony under oath, he denied having any knowledge of the extra tip-up. He stressed the tip-up was not his.

The judge found the man not guilty of the charge. The man stood up from the defendant table in the courtroom and walked to the exit door with a smile on his face. Before leaving the courtroom the man stopped at the door, turned to the judge and asked, "When do I get my tip-up back?"

The judge's face turned various shades of red as his anger rose. The judge knew the man had just made a fool out of him for believing his testimony instead of mine. The judge snarled, "Your tip-up?" He then screamed, "Get out of my courtroom!"

I quietly collected my reports and left the courtroom without saying anything. Eventually the judge began to believe my testimony more than the testimony of other defendants.

Some DNR cases brought before a judge are for more serious cases such as shining and shooting deer at night. A LaCrosse man was arrested for shining a deer with a spotlight and shooting the deer with a rifle on private land along the Jackson/LaCrosse county line. The landowner saw the violation take place and wrote down the license plate number of the vehicle.

The man had a unique explanation for his crime. He stated that he had been visiting his mother at her home in the area. On the way back to LaCrosse, he became lost on the side roads he was on. About that time he saw a deer in the field so he stopped to shine and shoot the deer because he was lost! The explanation didn't result in a lot of sympathy by the court. The judge in that case found the man guilty which included a large monetary penalty and the loss of DNR privileges for three years.

31 Fishing Without a License

A warden will check thousands of fishing licenses during a career. Wardens also write more citations for fishing without a license than any other violation. Through these thousands of contacts, it is inevitable that not all of these contacts will be routine.

It is human nature to feel nervous, scared, or apprehensive when an individual realizes they are about to be caught fishing without a license. Most people have the same reaction when the red and blue lights come on behind them when they are speeding on the interstate. Wardens recognize that receiving a citation is not a positive part of the person's day.

People react in a lot of different ways. A few men, usually from the Chicago area, wouldn't even take the time to look at me when I asked to see their fishing license. They would simply open their wallet while they kept fishing, and would hand me their driver's license with a $50 bill underneath. I would alert the men that they had mistakenly handed me the money with their driver's license and would hold the large bill out to them so they could take it back. I don't know what goes on in their home communities, but the men always seemed surprised I was returning the $50. They were even more disappointed when I issued the citation for fishing without a license.

Other people were a little more creative. Some unlicensed anglers will attempt to give an alias instead of their real name. In some of these situations, this would only last until I ran a check on the people and found the alleged name to not be on file. However one man actually gave me the name and date of birth of his brother. When a warrant was issued for failure to pay the bond or to appear in court, I went to the address listed on the citation and contacted the brother who obviously knew nothing

135

about what had happened. The brother who had been fishing was then charged for obstructing an officer for giving false information. I can only guess what the innocent brother gave his brother for punishment.

A few people would not hesitate when I approached to check their fishing licenses. Some would simply attempt to flee the scene. I recall one of these situations as I approached two older teenagers fishing in the Bark River east of Fort Atkinson. I was 50 yards away from them, approaching on foot, when the young men threw their fishing rods in the river and took off running in the opposite direction. I gave chase despite their head start.

They were surprised when I caught up to them after more than a 200 yard sprint. I ran up between them as they ran side by side, and put a hand on each of their shoulders and told them they were under arrest. Gasping for breath, the young men sat down on a log and pulled out a pack of cigarettes to have a smoke. I was still in my 20's and in good shape, but I doubt I would have caught them with my heavy duty belt on if they had not been smokers.

On another occasion, a woman tried to shift the fishing responsibilities to a child in her vehicle. However, I drew the line when the woman pointed at tip-ups in front of her truck on Lake Koshkonong claiming they belonged to her son. Her son was less than 18 months old and was strapped in a car seat. I told the woman to pull the lines and go home.

The strangest response I received when I asked to see a fishing license; came on a warm sunny day on Rock Lake in Jefferson County. A man and a woman dressed in a two piece swim suit were both fishing from a boat that I approached with my patrol boat. The woman did not have a fishing license. After asking for some identification, I informed the woman that I would be issuing a citation to her for fishing without a license.

As I was writing the citation just a few feet away from the woman, she asked if there was some other way we could take care of this. I looked up to see that the woman had untied her bikini top and was barely holding it over strategic areas. Surprising as that sounds; the man in the boat she was fishing with didn't pay any attention to her special offer to me. He just kept fishing. I declined the woman's offer and issued the citation. One can only guess what she was planning.

32 Every Day Has Risks

There is no typical day in law enforcement. I found over more than 30 years of law enforcement work that I was unable to predict what any day was going to be like when I left my home. That is why law enforcement officers sometimes linger a second or two when they say goodbye to their spouse or children before walking out to their police car or warden truck.

During my career, some of the most dangerous experiences took place on what I had planned to be administrative or office days. I shared one of those experiences with a young warden on a day we simply planned to visit the area DNR office in Madison. When we completed our business there, we began traveling eastbound on Highway 18 towards Jefferson County. Shortly after we left Madison, we heard an officer calling for immediate assistance on a county road that intersected with Highway 18. I asked Mike to pull out our road atlas to see how far away that county road was from us in Dane County. The words were hardly out of my mouth when I said to Mike, "Forget it, we are already here."

A county sheriff's squad car was parked on the side of the road behind another vehicle about 75 yards to our right on the county road. We pulled in behind him and activated our emergency lights. He was happy to see us. The deputy informed us that he had been pursuit of a man who had attempted to kidnap a young girl who had been riding her bicycle down the road. She had managed to escape the man. The deputy also explained that the man was recently paroled from prison for the rape of another woman. The deputy stated that once the vehicle had been stopped, the man ran from the vehicle into a wooded area across the road.

I suggested to the deputy that we go into the woods after the guy. He then added that the man was armed with a 270 caliber rifle. I acknowledged that this fact changed the situation. I looked slightly behind us to our left and noticed a residence in the same woodlot the man had run into. I told the deputy that Mike and I were going to drive up to the front door to warn the occupants to stay inside and to lock all of their doors. Mike and I then drove up to the house and told some young people inside not to go near any windows and to stay behind locked doors. We then drove back to park behind the deputy.

A swarm of other squad cars then descended on the scene. As other police cars pulled up, we thought we heard one or two rifle shots from the wooded valley below. Everyone was crouched down behind cover wondering who or what the man was shooting at. This began a tense 3 hour waiting game. A police negotiator began to call to the suspect on a loudspeaker encouraging him to surrender. There was no response during these three hours of waiting. As Mike and I hid behind the vehicles, I pointed out to him how other officers were responding to the situation. I told him to look at one officer from another agency that had climbed ten feet up the hillside adjacent to all the squads to hide behind a wood fence post. I suggested to Mike that the 3 inch diameter cedar post was not going to stop a 270 rifle round.

With no response at all from the suspect, a police dog and swat team members eventually moved into the wooded area. The suspect was then found to be dead from a self-inflicted gunshot wound. As we drove the rest of the way back to Jefferson at the end of the incident, it was a stark reminder that none of us has any idea what we may encounter on any given day that we wear a badge.

33 Above the Law

It was the last day of the Buffalo County deer gun season in 2004. Closing time on the last Sunday had passed. Bob dropped me off at my truck so I could begin my hour drive home. As I started to drive southbound along the river, I began to mentally unwind. Wardens are always happy to see the end of another deer gun season. I could now begin to anticipate more normal days ahead without armed confrontations or hunting accidents.

Unfortunately, my brief respite from deer season stress was short-lived. Even though darkness had fallen over the forest, one property owner apparently felt he was entitled to hunt after hours after everyone else had stopped hunting. The Sheriff's department dispatcher called for Bob and I to respond to a shooting in progress call on a very large property that was privately owned. The complainant advised they were hearing rifle shots from a vehicle they could see being driven across a field. It was now more than 25 minutes after closing time.

Due to where I was at that moment, I knew I would be closest to the complaint. In fact I was straight west of the property when the call came in. I turned inland from the Mississippi River and began to prepare myself mentally for the unknown. This was no time to relax. I had to be on top of my game. I was going to be driving into a large piece of private property where I had never been before. I would be driving in to confront one or more armed hunters in the dark who knew they were violating the law. I hoped that Bob would not be far behind.

I found the driveway into the property and turned left on to the land from the county road. Fortunately, the owner had not closed the gate so I was able to respond in my truck rather than on foot. Several hundred yards from the highway I observed a cabin. I also could see a vehicle with its lights on up the hill to my left. In the darkness I now had to figure out how to get to the vehicle. A deep ravine ran through the property. I had to find the correct forest trail to cross the ravine from. After reaching one dead end, I quickly turned around and found a lane that led to the suspect's vehicle. The vehicle's headlights had been turned off for a period of time suggesting the suspects did not want to be found.

I parked with my headlights pointing at two hunters standing outside the open vehicle doors. Dead deer lay on the ground behind the vehicle. I observed a bloody knife on the front seat. The man and woman were frantically searching the back of their hunting coats for a deer tag. I identified myself as a warden and asked the two hunters for some identification. At that point, Bob also arrived on scene.

The man was the landowner and asked what we wanted. I discussed the concern over the late shots. The man was quite belligerent and stated that those violations do not apply to private land. He then added that a deceased warden had told him shooting crippled deer after hours was legal. I informed the man that was not the case.

When I asked who shot the doe behind the truck they advised the wife had. I asked the man's wife if she knew what time hunting hours had ended. She replied that she did not. I asked her if she knew what time it was now and she again replied that she did not. She then advised she had been able to see the doe to shoot it. I asked the woman to show me where the doe was shot, while Bob talked to the man.

The woman directed me across the valley to a picked cornfield. She showed me where to drive my truck to get there. When I asked her how she had shot her deer, she explained that she had got out of their truck and had shot over the hood of the vehicle. There was snow on the ground in the field so I walked along the vehicle's tire tracks looking for footprints. There were no footprints in the snow until the vehicle's occupants had left the vehicle to pick up the deer. In other words, the deer had been shot from inside the truck and due to the time the shots were fired, the two hunters had likely shined the deer with the vehicle's headlights. The woman denied all of this and suggested that her footprints were there but that I couldn't find them. The woman also could not explain why there were no shell casings in the field where she had supposedly shot while on foot.

I drove the woman back to our original location and stopped to talk with Bob about what I had found. He filled me in on what he had discovered. Bob explained that the doe the woman had shot was not tagged, despite the fact it had been loaded up into the truck and transported away from the scene. The buck that was next to the doe on the ground was not tagged until the man tagged it while Bob investigated an illegal bait pile. The buck had been shot over an illegal bait pile in another field. Hunters are only allowed up to 2 gallons of corn at a bait site, and this particular corn pile was at least 7 or 8 gallons in size. Bob also explained that the man had shot the doe to finish it off even though he did not possess a deer gun license.

Bob and I discussed all the violations with the man and his wife. The man responded that these were "technical" violations that should not apply to private land. We informed the man and wife that criminal charges could be issued in this case but that we were instead going to issue citations for failure to immediately tag a deer and for hunting deer over illegal bait. After taking care of the paperwork, I was finally able to continue my trip home ending a 15 hour day.

Most people try to learn from their mistakes. Usually after someone is cited for hunting violations, they try harder to comply with the law in the future. However this landowner did not fit that mold. The following year we received information that the same man had a very large pile of shell corn lying on the ground behind his cabin. We looked down the valley towards the cabin from a town road high on the ridge. Even from a distance of a quarter mile away, the corn pile was clearly visible. We knew we would have to visit the camp again since it was now another deer gun season.

When we attempted to enter the camp the second year, we found the gate at the entrance of the property to be locked. Apparently, the owner did not want any more uninvited warden visits. We decided to walk in on foot. We encountered the man's son and daughter-in-law. They were in possession of a buck the woman had just shot. However the deer was tagged with her husband's tag. The man was not hunting and did not have a weapon or blaze orange clothing with him in the field. This was a violation of the group hunting law because a hunter can only tag a deer for someone else if the other person is actively hunting. We then decided to issue one citation for the group hunting violation but did not seize the deer.

We asked about the large pile of shell corn behind the cabin. The son stated the corn was from the cornfield that had been picked before the deer gun season. We informed him that the pile would have to be covered to make it inaccessible to deer since it was acting as a gigantic bait pile. There was enough corn on the ground to fill a farmer's gravity box or a small dump truck. Bob also called the landowner on the phone to inform him of the same requirements.

Two deer seasons later, Bob again informed me that a large pile of corn was again outside the man's cabin. Once again we entered the property to address the corn pile. We knew that every night deer would be feeding on the corn. This would attract deer from the surrounding area to the man's property which was illegal. It also gave his hunting group an unfair advantage over legal hunters on adjacent lands. As we entered the property, I saw that a hunter in a well-built enclosed stand to my right had just shot a buck. I walked out to the hunter while Bob continued forward to the cabin. The hunter in the blind came outside as I approached. I found the woman to be the landowner's daughter. I checked her hunting license and asked if she needed help tagging the deer. She advised that her dad takes care of tagging issues. I wondered what that meant. I congratulated the woman on her buck and walked up to the cabin.

The landowner drove up to the cabin and started screaming at me. He was very belligerent again and was ranting about wardens being on his land again. When I saw the man approaching I turned on the tape recorder on my gun belt. Documenting what takes place with this kind of person can be very valuable later in court. The man's daughter walked up to the cabin as the man screamed at me some more. I finally told the man that his daughter had just shot a nice buck. I asked him if he really wanted to ruin his daughter's experience this way. That seemed to shut him up for a while.

Bob and I then explained that the huge pile of corn could not be left on the ground during the hunting season to draw in deer. The man said it was a normal farming practice. I told the man that farmers don't dump a truck load of shell corn for deer to eat the week of the deer season as part of a normal farming practice. Bob again told the man to put a tarp or something else over it to keep it inaccessible to deer. The man argued that the corn wasn't dry yet so he couldn't tarp it. I told the man that if the corn wasn't dry yet, other farmers would have allowed the corn to mature in the field before picking. I told him the corn should not to be picked simply because it was deer season.

The man was then advised he would be getting an illegal feeding citation for continuing to engage in this activity even though he had been directed not to do this in the past. The man remained quite hostile. Bob and I then left the property.

The following fall another member of the man's family was cited for hunting over a large illegal bait pile during the archery season. After that arrest, complaints continued to come in of the landowner hauling loads of corn to tree stands with his John Deere Gator.

I doubt that this man will ever change his ways. He is a very wealthy man who believes that he should be able to buy anything or to do anything he wants. He is not accustomed to people holding him accountable because in normal day to day life he gets his way. The man is well-connected politically; hosting events for candidates for high office at his business. He probably thinks that with his connections and political appointees running the DNR, he should be untouchable. Based on his actions with us over several deer seasons, we feel that he believes he is above the law.

However if game wardens are going to uphold the public trust, they must treat all people the same way. A large bank account or political affiliation should not dictate whether or not someone needs to follow the deer hunting regulations. If all men are truly created equal in this country, then the laws should apply equally to all.

34 The Painful Buck

I was northbound on Highway 35 on my way home to LaCrosse. It was a weekday during the deer gun season. Closing hours for deer hunters had passed as it was now well after dark. While I was driving up the highway with my headlights on, I noticed a truck parked along the road in an area north of Goose Island that was open to deer hunting. I wondered why the hunter was still in the woods.

I turned off the highway and parked my truck behind the hunter's truck. I slowly climbed out of my truck before quietly closing the truck door. Walking slowly forward in the dark, I took a few steps in the dark and listened. I kept my flashlight off as was customary when a warden was trying to gather information as to what may be going on at a location. By walking in the dark, I was not going to alert hunters or poachers that someone was near.

A small stream passed under the highway and flowed into the hunting area. A footpath extended into the woods along the stream that hunters often followed. I began to slowly feel my way down the path into the woods. As I again stopped to listen, I immediately became concerned.

I could hear a man moaning. I heard a few twigs snap and then heard more moaning. I feared that a man had been shot and was trying to reach his vehicle to get help. I turned on my flashlight and quickly walked towards the sound of the moans. I soon observed a hunter dressed in blaze orange doubled over in pain. Surprisingly the man was also dragging a nice buck.

I identified myself as a conservation warden and asked the man if he was hurt. The man dropped the rope he was holding that was attached to the buck. He then struggled to stand up straight. The man caught his breath and finally began to speak.

"I am hurt but not in the way you think. Two days ago I had a vasectomy. I should have thought about that before I shot this stupid deer. It took me 2 hours of dragging in pain to get this buck out to the road!" I nodded my head in sympathy, appreciating the fact this was one self-inflicted injury that would not require a hunting accident report.

35 Lessons in Life from the Potato Patch

No matter what kind of law enforcement training an officer receives, there is always a bit of instinct that kicks in during a stressful situation in which we tap into something that we may have learned earlier in life. For some of us that may be a technique learned in high school wrestling or football. For others, it could be past military training. For me it was a lesson passed on to me from my grandfather.

During my youth I spent many hours working with my grandfather in a very large potato patch in his garden. Each year I would help him to plant and later harvest more than a thousand hills of potatoes. This work took many hours to accomplish so it provided an opportunity for many hours of discussions on a wide range of topics.

We were working in the garden when I was around 20 years old when my grandfather took it upon himself to teach me the ways of the world. I kept digging as he talked fearing the uncertainty of where this was going to lead. It wasn't what you might expect. Grandfather told me he wanted me to be aware of what I needed to know about box socials.

Box socials I asked? Grandfather related that the church he attended during his teen years held an annual box social to raise funds for worthy causes. The single young women would prepare a variety of baked goods which were then placed in a box with their name on it. Single young men could then bid on the baked goods.

Apparently there were some unwritten rules involving who bid on what as my grandfather discovered. My grandfather purchased the goods from one young lady's donated parcel only to find out that her boyfriend was not impressed with the competition who outbid him. Baking abilities alone did not dictate how vigorous the bidding went. Boyfriends were always supposed to buy their girlfriend's baked goods.

After all the bidding was done, the boyfriend and two of his buddies came after my grandfather to correct the social transgression. It was then that he shared some advice that I could use. Grandfather suggested that if in a fight with more than one guy, you want to have your back to a corner. That way no one can get at you from behind. He also added that when someone comes after you, try to grab them by the hair since you can control the movement of their entire body when you are steering them from the head. These tactics helped grandfather get out of the box social in one piece.

Many years later in June of 1992, I was on the Mississippi River working in my job as a conservation warden. Another warden and I were on the river with our patrol boat when we observed a motorboat being operated on the main channel of the river after sunset without navigation lights. When we activated our blue flashing police lights, the man took a quick turn into a side slough to evade us. The boat operator looked directly at us several times but refused to stop.

When we maneuvered our patrol boat alongside the suspect's boat to try to obtain boat registration numbers, we found that numbers were not displayed as required. Therefore we had no idea who owned the boat or who was operating it. The man was steering his boat around blind corners without boat lights at a high rate of speed. We feared he was going to collide with another boat or would run over an anchored fisherman.

As the man drove farther into the backwaters south of

LaCrosse, we were concerned how this pursuit was going to end. We pursued the man with our patrol boat until the man finally ran aground with his boat in a shallow side slough. While the man's boat suddenly stopped from the motor's lower unit plowing into the bottom, our boat had the motor trimmed up so it continued flying forward towards a wall of cattails. Not willing to wait for the impact, I leaped from our patrol boat, landing on the hard sand bottom. I then waded towards the suspect boat. A minute later the other warden followed me.

The man was totally uncooperative both verbally and physically. He was also very intoxicated. Empty beer cans littered the bottom of the boat. The man refused to give his name. We were unable to use our patrol boat to transport the man because it was solidly lodged behind a wall of cattails. As the other warden and I pushed the man's boat back to deeper water to transport him to a waiting Sheriff's boat, the man continued to resist by pushing the outboard motor down into the water against us. I finally grabbed the man by his hair and pulled him face down into the bottom of the boat to subdue him. I then placed the man in handcuffs.

When we reached the Sheriff's patrol boat, the deputies transported the prisoner with me to a boat landing where a squad car could take us to the Sheriff's department. Meanwhile, my partner had to recruit 4 men from a campsite along the river to help him to extricate our patrol boat from the cattails.

When we processed the man at the county jail, he refused to take the preliminary breath test and emphasized that point by spitting on the informing the accused form. The man was issued citations for multiple charges and spent the rest of the night in jail. Later he would be served a criminal complaint for obstructing an officer that led to 30 days in the county jail with

Huber privileges.

As the other warden and I ended our shift later in the evening, the other warden asked me where I learned to take down a man by grabbing him by the hair. I simply replied "That is the way Grandpa D would have done it." The warden suggested "You can't do that," concerned there was some potential conflict with the use of force policy. I never gave it another thought.

Seven months later, the same warden and I were at the State Patrol Academy together for our annual in-service training. Each winter we had to attend to maintain our law enforcement certification. Usually there would be a legal update as well as self-defense training. During this particular winter session, we were told we had a new defensive tactics instructor to teach new innovative techniques in controlling offenders who were resisting arrest. We were told these new tactics were such that they would not hurt us or the people we needed to subdue. The instructor was a new citizen of the United States who had worked in the Soviet Union. There were some not so subtle suggestions he had been a member of the KGB or Russian secret police.

He could speak fairly good English and taught us some good techniques. The very first thing he demonstrated to us was to "hook them up" which meant grabbing the adversary by the hair and pulling him down to the ground. The other warden's jaw dropped in disbelief as he looked at me, because he remembered how I had used the same technique on the intoxicated boater. I just smiled and thought to myself that this is nothing new. Grandfather taught me that technique many years ago. I wonder if they have box socials in Russia.

Steven Dewald